For all the Saints
Who from their labors rest

Allison Nelson
Maria Almet
Erwin Panjaitan

Acknowledgments

It is plain from the text that this book is not the work of a single author. My intention at the beginning was to let Indonesians speak for themselves as much as possible. Were I still living in Indonesia at the time I put this book together, this goal would have been more attainable. As it is, I have relied on materials that were for the most part written collectively during the course of nearly twelve years' work in Indonesia. The case study method that forms the backbone of this book was developed and introduced to Indonesia by my colleague, friend, and mentor, Dr. Tjaard G. Hommes. The contributors include theological professors and students, pastors and lay persons—and of course the farmers, factory workers, homemakers, and villagers who actually lived out the stories we have recorded and commented upon. Their names have been separated from the case studies to which they contributed for the sake of confidentiality. Here I wish to record their names along with my heartfelt thanks. They are Nicodemus and Petrus Almet, Pao Ina Bara Pah, Aleta Baun, Mess Beeh, Peter Hancock, Anne and Tjaad Hommes, Junus Inabuy, Timur Indyah, Arlindo Marçal, Thobias Messakh, Semuel Nitti, Judo Poerwowidagdo, Ayub Ranoh, M. E. Simorangkir, Gerrit Singgih, Bendalina Souk, Robert Tahun, Tom Therik, Nico Woly, and Andreas Yewangoe.

Of course I take full responsibility for any errors or misrepresentations contained in the text. The Indonesian tradition is to ask forgiveness for anything that may have caused offense, and I do so now: *Maafkan saya apabila ada yang menyinggung perasaan.*

I also owe thanks to Susan Converse Winslow of Friendship Press for her guidance and encouragement, and to the two congregations I serve: Robbins Memorial Congregational Church and Whately Congregational Church, both of the United Church of Christ, for their kindness and patience in allowing me the time to write this book. Finally, I thank my family with a sense of gratitude that only a loving family can teach us: Karen; Katie; Sam; my mother, Inena Nelson; and the Almet clan of Lelobatan, Timor.

The figure on the title page is a carved leather puppet from traditional Javanese puppet theater. The chapter heads, drawn by Paul Lansdale, are taken from batik (Introduction, chapters 2, 4, 8), basketry (chapter 3), silver work (chapter 5), stone carving (chapter 6), wood carving (chapter 7), and burned bamboo work (conclusion), from various Indonesian islands.

Indonesia
in Shadow and Light

John Campbell-Nelson

Friendship Press • New York

Copyright © 1998 Friendship Press

Editorial Offices:
475 Riverside Drive, New York, NY 10115

Distribution Offices:
P.O. Box 37844, Cincinnati, Ohio 45222-0844

Manufactured in the United States of America

Library of Congress Cataloging-in-Publication Data

Campbell-Nelson, John.
    Indonesia in shadow and light / John Campbell-Nelson.
        p.   cm.
    Includes bibliographical references.
    ISBN 0-377-00321-2
    1. Indonesia I. Title.
DS615.C35   1998
959.8—dc21
                                             97-37534
                                               CIP

Contents

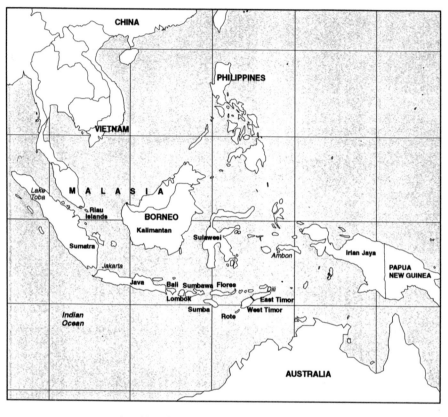

INDONESIA

Introduction

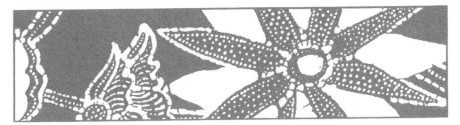

Near a beach in Kupang, the port city and provincial capital of Timor in eastern Indonesia, is a fresh-water spring known locally as Oeba. During the dry season, when water slows to a trickle in the city's pipes, women come here to wash their laundry and gossip, and children come to bathe and play after the heat of the day. It was here in 1789 that William Bligh ended his long journey by small boat across the Pacific after the mutiny on the *Bounty*. He was welcomed by the Dutch, who had maintained a trading post in Kupang for nearly two hundred years, exchanging small quantities of European manufactured goods for large quantities of sandalwood and beeswax.

The Dutch were the latest in a long line of foreign merchants who had sought the fragrant wood for which the island is famous. Traders from India arrived in about the first or second century A.D. They were followed over the centuries by the Chinese, Javanese, Arabs, Portuguese, and finally the Dutch. Each brought something new to the island: necklaces of Indian beads are still exchanged in marriage ceremonies (much as Westerners use wedding rings); centuries-old Chinese pottery is still in use; the Portuguese brought indigo dye and cloth, horses, papaya, tobacco, and most important of all, maize (corn), which soon became the staple food of the Timorese. Although most of these merchant powers had at one time or another claimed Timor as a vassal or colony, the designation meant little to the Timorese. They simply divided their unruly guests into *kais muti* and *kais metan*—"white strangers" and "black strangers"—who had come bringing interesting and sometimes useful objects to barter. For three hundred years, until the early part of the twentieth century, Dutch influence was largely confined to Kupang, where their garrison and fort served not as a base from which to rule the island but (as Bligh shrewdly observed in his journal) "as a Secure Retreat for the Europeans in case of an insurrection."

Bligh wandered about Kupang while awaiting a ship to take him on to England. In the marketplace he noticed the large number of people who brought tiny quantities of tobacco, betel nut, oranges, onions, garlic, and yams for sale or trade. "I have seen a man bring only two Potatoes to sell, which being bought for halfpenny, he has immediately laid [his money] out for betel and lounged the remaining part of the day around the Town. This is not a singular instance but gives the real Character of the Whole people." What Bligh saw as endemic laziness and ignorance of commerce was (and still is) to the Timorese a cherished form of sociability.

In due course Bligh was taken to pay a state visit to the Timorese "Kaiser" of Kupang. What seems to have made the greatest impression on him was a new dish he was served: "The Indian corn by the mode of dressing it turned the Grains inside out, every Grain begins to burst and fly about," although the finished product is "perhaps the most tempting pretty Dish that can be put upon a Table." Today it is available at every movie theater; we call it popcorn.

Amused and bemused, Bligh is like most of us when we encounter a culture radically different from our own. Much of the time we don't know what we are seeing, and when we think we do, we are often wrong. Occasionally we see things that the local people do not. Engulfed in novelty, we are constantly trying to interpret what we see while being forced to suspend judgment. We seek to understand the new in light of what we already know, and often that is not enough.

Most of us in North America know very little about the vast and complex nation of Indonesia, partly because it is so far away, almost exactly on the opposite side of the globe, and mostly in the Southern Hemisphere. Until recently, we have had relatively little contact, trade, or diplomatic interest, at least not of the sort that makes front-page news. For most Americans, "Java" is a cup of coffee, not the island that gave it its name. That has begun to change as "Made in Indonesia" now appears on the collars of our shirts and the lining of our shoes, or as we have seen news footage of President Clinton appearing in traditional batik cloth with Indonesian President Suharto at an Asia-Pacific Economic Cooperation (APEC) meeting. Or perhaps some of us saw the terrifying images of a massacre of East Timorese civilians in 1991 by the Indonesian military. During the tourist boom of the 1970s and 1980s, increasing numbers of Americans and Canadians discovered the elegant hotels and sunny beaches of Bali. For the most part, however, our knowledge of Indonesia is slight compared to its vast size and its increasing importance as an economic and political power on the Pacific rim. This book is intended to make a small contribution toward correcting that historical oversight.

Why should North Americans know more about Indonesia? Often the quickest way to catch someone's attention when talking about Indonesia ("What? Where's that? Don't you mean India?") is with a few statistics. Here are a few, by way of introduction:

- Indonesia is the world's fourth largest country by population. With just over 200 million people, it is next largest to the United States.
- It has the world's largest Muslim population, with more Muslims than all the Arab countries combined. Christianity is the second largest religion, with more than 20 million adherents.
- It includes about 400 distinct ethnic groups, each with its own language. (The national language is called Bahasa Indonesia, a variation of Malay.)
- By size, Indonesia is about as large as the United States, although most of its area is water. It includes half of the second largest island in the world (New Guinea), most of the third largest (Borneo), and all of the sixth largest (Sumatra). In all, there are either 13,000 or 17,000 or 20,000 islands—they are still counting, thanks to improved satellite imaging.

Americans will likely experience a study of Indonesia as a study in contrasts, both within the country itself and with the United States. Both countries had a large and diverse indigenous population at the time when European colonization began. In 1597 the Dutch East Indies Company founded a trading post in Java called Batavia, which has now grown to a city of nearly 12 million people, better known as Jakarta. Some years later in 1625 their sister corporation, the Dutch West Indies Company, set up a trading post called Nieuw Amsterdam, which has now grown to a city of about 16 million people, better known as New York. The subsequent histories, of course, are very different indeed, but when independence came to the two countries, they chose almost the same motto. The United States' *E Pluribus Unum* is matched by Indonesia's *Bhinneka Tunggal Ika*, which is usually translated as "Unity in Diversity." The diversity of Indonesia is far greater than that of the United States, and it is of a different nature. Whereas European immigrants gradually pushed aside and nearly exterminated the indigenous peoples of the North American continent, there was never any large-scale immigration of Europeans to the Indonesian archipelago. The diversity of Indonesia today is almost entirely composed of indigenous peoples who retain an ancestral homeland within the country. It is painful to imagine what might have been had America followed this course.

So why study Indonesia? Because of the 200 million people or the 20,000 islands, because of the increasing links with North America in trade and international politics; because Christians are afraid of Islam and there are so many Muslims there? Or perhaps because American and Canadian churches have formed partnerships with Indonesian churches just as our corporations have formed partnerships with their Indonesian counterparts, and therefore we need to know our partners? Maybe it is because we like to wear shoes that happen to be sewn in Indonesian sweatshops by workers paid $2.25 a day?

I studied Indonesia initially because I had a job there as a missionary. I was called by the Evangelical Protestant Church of Timor and sent by the United Church Board for World Ministries of the United Church of Christ. My wife and I wanted to experience what it is like to be a Christian in a radically different cultural context, and at the time it didn't much matter to us where we went, as long as it promised maximum difference from the United States. After nearly twelve years there, I find that I am still studying Indonesia, but my reasons have changed. I study it because it is like discovering another world that is strange and terrible and wonderful, that can expand my conception of God's creation and of the human possibilities it promises. That is a lofty sentiment, sincerely expressed. Yet I cannot let it stand without adding that many of my Indonesian friends would respond to it with only an ironic smile. Kartini, a Javanese noblewoman who advocated women's right to an education at the beginning of the twentieth century, once wrote of a Dutch admirer:

> The professor thought we were partial savages and discovered ordinary people; what was strange was only skin color, clothing, and environment, and these gave a peculiar cachet to the ordinary. Don't we feel pleasantly moved when we discover our own thought in another person? And if the other is a stranger, someone of a different race, from a different continent, different blood, color, mores and customs, then this can only enhance the attraction of spiritual congeniality.

Kartini was acutely aware that it is no complement to be considered exotic. But she was gracious enough and wise to point to the true prize: the discovery of our common humanity.

This book is intended to introduce the reader to some of the main social, economic, and political dynamics in modern Indonesia, with special reference to their implications for the life and work of the Christian churches there. There are several biases and shortcomings to this approach that you should know about from the beginning. First, the Christian perspective means that you will be seeing the country largely through the eyes of a minority group, although you will hear a few Muslim voices here as well. Christians account for 10 to 15 percent of the population, and they are very unevenly distributed geographically. The influence of Islam was most strongly felt in Java and the coastal areas of Sumatra, Sulawesi, and Kalimantan (the Indonesian portion of Borneo). The central highlands of the latter three islands as well as most of eastern Indonesia were relatively untouched by foreign religions until the coming of the Dutch. Through missionary activity most of these areas are now chiefly Christian, although the influence of indigenous ("tribal") religion is still strongly felt. For this reason I shall give as much attention to the interaction of Christianity with indigenous religion as to Christian-Muslim relations, and eastern Indonesia is better represented than the more populous Java.

Second, although the locus of political and economic change is primarily in the cities, two thirds of the population live in rural areas. It is here that the environmental and social effects of national development are most acutely felt. Accordingly, rural life will be more the focus of attention than life in the cities.

Finally, I have tried to reach a compromise between those issues likely to be of most concern to North American readers and the priorities of Indonesian Christians themselves. Problems of church development and polity are less in evidence here than they would be had I followed the agenda of many Indonesian Christians. Issues of institutional survival are no less an obsession in Indonesian churches than in the United States and Canada.

The plan of this book is based on the case study method as it was introduced and developed by my colleague Dr. Tjaard G. Hommes in a series of writers' workshops given over a ten-year period in a wide variety of settings throughout Indonesia. The writers included Indonesian pastors, theologians, and interested lay persons who brought many years of experience in trying to live out their Christian faith in the Indonesian context. Our challenge was to stimulate a new kind of theological reflection, one that would be rooted in the participants' own experience as Indonesian Christians, and free either to use or to set aside the Western theologies that had been so dominant in their history as "mission churches." For this reason we took as our starting point neither doctrine nor the Bible but the actual stories and struggles of the Indonesian people. We used the case study method as a way of bringing these experiences into dialogue with the broader Christian tradition.

Case studies are a useful tool for reflecting on the complexities of human experience in a disciplined way. The method is as simple or complicated as you care to make it, but the basic pattern is this: Tell a story that is significant, problematic, or puzzling enough that you want to understand it better. Tell the story simply, clearly, and in enough detail that people who have not been part of the actual events can enter into the dynamics of the story. Then stand back and look at this story, or case, much as a detective might, in order to try to understand what happened and why it happened as it did. Like the detective, you are interested in the motives, perceptions, and emotions of the actors in the case, and how they are affected by social, economic and cultural factors. Also like the detective, you must base your conclusions on evidence drawn from the case itself. Next, ask yourself what it all means. This is where moral and religious perspectives come into play: What values are at stake here? What does your religious faith have to say about it? How does it challenge your faith and your values? Finally, ask what, if anything, should be done about it. It is crucial to follow these steps in order, or you will find yourself quite literally "jumping to conclusions," and you will learn nothing new. In the language of the case study method, these four steps are called description, analysis, interpretation, and action. They can be put most simply as a series of four questions:

- Description: What happened?
- Analysis: Why did it happen that way?
- Interpretation: What does it mean for our faith and values?
- Action: What should we do about it?

Except for the historical introduction, most of the chapters in this book are adapted from case studies actually written by Indonesian Christians. As case studies they inevitably focus more on the problems than the achievements of Indonesia, a fact that in no way diminishes the dedication of the writers to their country. Many of the stories were originally published in the Indonesian language as part of the Pastoral Case Studies series sponsored by the Institute for Advanced Pastoral

Studies of the Southeast Asian Graduate School of Theology, whose permission to republish them here is gratefully acknowledged. I have added introductions and explanatory notes as necessary to make them intelligible to the North American reader. Additional materials that give another perspective or expand upon the themes of the case studies appear in separate sections in the text. My goal has been to intrude as little as possible, to stand aside and let Indonesians tell their own story. In order to maintain confidentiality in pastoral situations (and occasionally to avoid possible political reprisals), the names of both case writers and actors in the cases themselves have been changed.

I suggest that you read this book in the same way that it was written. Read the story first, and ask yourself the four questions above. Then go on reading to see how the Indonesian writer responded to this situation. It may be quite different from what you had imagined. In any event, the point is not to decide who is right and who is wrong but to learn from our differing perspectives.

Chapter 1

The Making of Indonesia

Indonesia is in many ways an improbable country. Its 200 million people speak hundreds of languages and inhabit thousands of islands. Stretching more than 3,000 miles from west to east, it covers a geographic area roughly the width of the United States, although most of it is water. Some of its peoples formed ancient kingdoms that rose to power soon after the time of the Roman Empire, yet it is considered a "new" nation, having gained its independence from the Dutch in the period of decolonization following World War II. Its modern boundaries derive more from its colonial past as the Dutch East Indies than from any obvious ethnic or geographic unity.

There is no simple way to introduce such a country. One must generalize, of course, but always with the warning that each generalization hides a multitude of exceptions and complexities. Almost every general statement could be completed with "Yes, but . . ." A few examples: Indonesia has its own airplane factory, but most of its citizens have never ridden in an airplane; in some areas many people have never ridden in an automobile. Indonesia is tremendously rich in natural resources, but the exploitation of these resources has caused intense social conflict and perilous degradation of the environment. It is rapidly becoming a major industrial power in Southeast Asia, but millions of its people are subsistence farmers, working the soil with little more than a hoe and a machete. Be forewarned, then, that the realities are much more complex than they appear in this brief orientation. It will offer three different perspectives, without assuming that one is more important than another: geography, social structure, and history. The chapter will conclude with a snapshot of the situation today.

The Land

There is a story told to children about how Indonesia came to be: In the beginning, the Creator took clay in his hands (yes, it's a "he"—these are mostly patriarchal societies we'll be dealing with) and formed the earth, molding and placing each of the continents just where he wanted them. Then he took water and poured it over the whole thing, to start the plants growing and to form the rivers and seas. Finally, when he was finished, he had mud all over his hands, so he flicked off the remaining clay, thus producing (as a playful afterthought) the islands that we now call Indonesia—the world's largest archipelagic nation.

This creation story makes about as much sense as what actually happened, and it has the advantage of brevity. The geological origins of Indonesia begin with the push and pull of the Australian and Asian continental plates, which created a huge fissure in the earth's surface. On the "push" cycle, marine coral buckled upward, forming the southeastern part of the archipelago. On the "pull" cycle, molten rock boiled up from the earth's core and deposited a row of volcanic islands stretching from Sumatra in the west through Java and Bali, and on to Alor in the east and northward through Sulawesi and the Moluccas. About a fourth of the world's active volcanoes are located in Indonesia.

This complex geological origin may not mean much in the abstract, but the difference between coral and volcanic soil means a great deal if you are a farmer. It is why high in the mountains of Timor you will find beautiful fossils of ancient marine life (beautiful, that is, unless you are trying to eke out a living in the rough coral-laden soil). When Timorese Christians sing "Rock of Ages" in church, it is a coral rock of which they are singing. This soil differential is also why Java can sustain 150 million people and produce four rice crops a year in its rich volcanic soil. And it is why, as I write these paragraphs in Yogyakarta (in central Java), villages just to the north of me are being evacuated after the most recent eruption of Mt. Merapi, the same volcano that once destroyed a central Javanese kingdom in the eleventh century. Local mystics see today's eruptions as a sign that the empire of the current president, Suharto, is nearing its end as well. There will be more about that later.

This geological history accounts in part for the wealth of Indonesia's natural resources. Aside from large tracts of fertile volcanic soil, the country's mineral resources include oil and natural gas, coal, iron, tin, nickel, copper, gold, and silver. These resources are sheltered by one of the world's largest tropical rain forests (second after Brazil). Most of this mineral wealth is located in what have been called the Outer Islands—the great majority of Indonesia's land mass to the east and north of Java, as well as the California-sized island of Sumatra to the west.

The equator bisects Indonesia, and the equatorial climate brings average temperatures in the upper 80s Fahrenheit and a cycle of two seasons rather than four: a rainy season from December through March and a dry season from June through September. Agriculture is possible year-round, although in dry areas much depends on the availability of ground water for irrigation.

To speak of "Outer Islands" begs the question, "Out from where?" The answer is, of course, "Out from Java." With nearly 70 percent of Indonesia's population, much of the country's fertile land, the greatest share of its industry, a rich and ancient cultural heritage, and a central role in the history of the region, it is perhaps understandable that most depictions of Indonesia center on Java. (To gain an idea of the population density of Java in relation to the rest of the nation, imagine that about 60 percent of the people in the United States live in the state of Tennessee.) Since before the time of Christ, the Javanese have been practicing a labor-intensive, high-yield system of irrigated rice cultivation made possible by the combination of fertile volcanic soil and ample rainfall.

Traditional water buffalos plowing a rice paddy are often more efficient than a tractor, which tends to stick in the mud.

Successful agriculture is a key to the development of any civilization. If you have surplus food, that means you also have surplus labor that can be devoted to other pursuits. Perhaps this is why so many of the arts and other aspects of material culture that are distinctive of Indonesia are in fact Javanese: textile arts (batik), music (gamelan), puppet theater (*wayang kulit*), and monumental architecture (Borobudur and Prambanan). This is true also of the neighboring island of Bali, where the system of irrigated rice cultivation is also dominant. Successive waves of immigrants and refugees from Java eventually engulfed the indigenous population to such an extent that what we call Balinese culture today is in fact an evolution of early Javan culture.

Java's neighbors in the Outer Islands were no less capable than the Javanese; they just had to devote most of their lives to survival. Mountainous terrain, erratic rainfall, and less fertile soils have greatly limited the development of irrigated rice culture in these areas. The main form of agriculture here is swidden, better known as "slash and burn" or shifting cultivation. An area of the forest is cleared of trees, or the branches are trimmed back to let the sunlight in. The field is then burned off in order to fertilize the soil with ash, and seasonal crops are planted—usually maize, field rice, cassava, yams, and beans. At most it is possible to obtain two crops a year, and often only one. When soil fertility declines, the farmers move on to another area and let their old fields return to forest. This system provides a fairly reliable source of food with minimal damage to the ecosystem as long as there is plenty of land available so that old fields can be left fallow long enough to restore their fertility. There is, however, little surplus left for trade or to support other economic activities.

Staple food crops were traditionally supplemented by hunting and gathering. I first saw this system in action in 1984 when I traveled to the island of Alor to do a workshop on church development for village churches in the eastern half of the island. Over a period of four days two hundred people were fed with maize and rice from local gardens. Every night a group of men went into the forest with bow and arrow and returned in the morning with deer and wild pig. Those living near the sea returned with a fresh catch of fish.

During the Suharto era, this age-old pattern has been increasingly difficult to maintain owing to rapid population growth and expropriation of tribal lands by the government and the forest industry. More people and less land means that the cycle of shifting cultivation is accelerated, and the forest does not have time to recover before it is farmed again. Deforestation means erosion, and the soil fertility declines even more rapidly, so that a downward spiral ensues from forest to grassland to wasteland.

Considering the geographic configuration of population and raw materials, it is not surprising that when Indonesia began to industrialize, the great majority of industry was located in Java. If agriculture feeds people, minerals and forest products feed industry. Java had a large supply of surplus labor, and the Outer Islands had the raw materials. The pattern of mercantilism developed by the Dutch, who exported raw materials from the islands to be sold or manufactured for the benefit of Holland, remains the dominant one today: raw materials are shipped from the Outer Islands to be processed in the factories of Java, and the manufactured products are either exported or sold domestically for the profit of the manufacturer. Thus a miner in Sumatra might buy back his own bauxite in the form of a cooking pot made in Java. The extreme example of exploitation of the Outer Islands is Irian Jaya, the Indonesian portion of New Guinea. One of the world's largest copper and gold mines is located there, operated by the Freeport-McMoRan Company of Louisiana. There they have built a Little America to house their American staff, while Javanese technicians supervise the indigenous people, who provide the bulk of manual labor. Due to its rich natural resources, Irian Jaya has one of the highest gross domestic products (GDP) in Southeast Asia, yet it has one of the lowest per capita incomes. Since the resources are simply extracted and exported, the people of Irian Jaya experience little of the benefits. And the more they know of the world beyond their mountain valleys, the more they resent what is happening to them.

The pattern for Indonesia's modern development thus emerges from the basic features of its geography: The seas provide inexpensive transportation for sending the raw materials of the Outer Islands (as well as much fish) to the ports of Java. By selling raw materials to industrialized countries, Indonesia has raised much of the capital needed for its own industrialization; at the same time, the rice paddies of Java provide the food needed to support a large pool of cheap industrial labor. For these new factories to remain competitive it is deemed necessary to keep labor costs down. Therefore agricultural prices are depressed so that factory workers can eat cheaply, and factory owners do not have to pay them as much. In this way both Javanese farmers and factory workers are kept in a state of marginal poverty. As for the people of the Outer Islands, except for day laborers in mining and forestry, they are pretty much superfluous to the system.

Patterns of Living

The two different systems of agriculture described above, irrigated rice cultivation and swidden (shifting) cultivation, have contributed to the development of two very different types of society. The coastal areas, with their ready access to the sea for fishing and trade, produced yet a third type.

Centralized Kingdoms

To build and maintain irrigation canals requires a great deal of coordinated manual labor. Then to divide the water fairly and effectively as it passes from field to field demands a high degree of consensus (or brute power) among the entire community. Central Java developed a social structure that was built upon this mode of production. As noted above, surplus food equals surplus labor, which then enables the development of a class of artisans and artists, and a standing army. Thus, entire river basins were organized into a network of villages under the rule of a central authority. The *kraton*, or palace, became the center of the realm, patron of the arts, and the source from which emanated the power that was believed to guarantee the well-being of the people. In return, the people offered up their crops and their labor as tribute to the royalty. A highly centralized and hierarchical society thus developed on the stable base of wet rice agriculture. The system was so effective that the Dutch had only to impose themselves at the top of the hierarchy to assert their colonial authority. And they succeeded best when they left it at that. From this Javanese hierachical system, aided by the Dutch genius for bureaucracy, emerged the basic structure of government present in Indonesia today. The contemporary Indonesian province loosely corresponds to a Javanese kingdom, which is subdivided into regencies (feudal lordships), sub-districts, and villages. Power flows down the chain and tribute flows up. Extended families are consequently less important in maintaining social and economic security than patron-client relationships—what Americans would call "connections."

Indonesian Interludes

Sultan's palace in Jogjakarta, Java, suggests the luxurious formality of court life in centuries past.

Farming Villages

Societies based on shifting cultivation tend to be quite different from those in Java. Where food sources are more varied and less secure it is difficult to sustain large concentrations of people. The typical pattern is for shifting cultivators to spread out, establishing small hamlets that are home to a single extended family. This family, consisting of a patriarch, his wife and children, and his younger brothers and their wives and children as well as any unmarried sisters, forms both the basic social unit and the basic unit of agricultural production. Although individuals may have responsibility for particular garden plots, much of the farm work, food supply, and child care are shared in common. Typically a child will view all older women as "mother" or "sister" and all older men as "father" or "brother." My family was adopted into such a community in Timor, and never before or since have we felt such a sense of security. These are largely closed, self-sustaining economies, each family unit producing the majority of its basic needs.

The scattered hamlets in a given area tend to form a loose confederation, usually based on family ties with in-laws and distant cousins. Even where something resembling a kingdom developed (often under influence from Dutch efforts to impose the Javanese model), the family metaphor was still dominant—the king was more of a patriarch than a Javanese-style demigod. These communal or "tribal" societies can be very stable as long as they control enough land to sustain their agricultural base.

Coastal Communities

A third type of society is found along the coastal areas. These people are often descendants of migrants from other islands, and they view the sea not as a barrier separating them from others but as a highway. The same skills in boatbuilding and navigation that make fish a major part of their diet give them the opportunity to travel to other islands, and travel means trade. Living near the sea lanes also means that they are in frequent contact with outsiders. Thus coastal peoples have become the traders, entrepreneurs, and brokers of the new. Their societies tend to be more ethnically mixed and less tradition bound than those of their neighbors in the interior. Many of them have a tradition known in the Malay language as *rantau*—young men are expected, almost as a rite of passage, to travel abroad and gain new skills and experiences that they will then bring back to enrich the life of the community. The coastal societies have been historically important for disseminating foreign influences, including Islam, which many coastal peoples adopted from their Arab and Malay trading partners.

The three types of society outlined here were first described by a prominent sociologist of Indonesia, W. F. Wertheim, who was writing in the 1950s. Although life in Indonesia is rapidly changing, these basic social structures remain very much in evidence. As we turn to the history of Indonesia, it is well to remember that for millions of Indonesians, *adat*, the tradition "handed down from the ancestors," is far more significant than the ebb and flow of political power that Westerners call history. Ask a Batak of north central Sumatra for a history of his people and he'll give you a genealogy.

Early Kingdoms

In many respects the history of Indonesia is best seen as the story of commerce among hundreds of peoples, alternately bartering and battling with one another for the rich mineral and botanical resources these islands possess.

The story of the Spice Islands, as the Europeans called them, goes back a long way. The first specimen of *Homo erectus*, one of the forerunners of *Homo sapiens*, was found in Java in 1890 and has been dated at around 700,000 years old. Later discoveries indicate that "Java Man" may have shared the island for a time with other proto-humans. It is likely that the peoples of the Pacific and Australia passed first through the Indonesian archipelago in a great diaspora that stretched over tens of thousands of years. The present-day Malay population are relative latecomers, migrating from Indochina in successive waves beginning around 2500 B.C. Typically the newcomers occupied the coastal areas and displaced older inhabitants, who moved farther into the interior.

Through the centuries other peoples arrived from India, China, Arabia, and Europe. They came primarily to trade. The peoples of the islands received cloth, ceramics, metal tools, maize, and horses. Europeans, Arabs, and mainland Asians received sandalwood, cloves, nutmeg, pepper, rubber, and sugar—the list is a long one.

The islands now known as Indonesia first appear in written records in the first century A.D. According to court annals, Chinese Emperor Wang Mang (A.D. 1–23) of the Han dynasty sent an expedition to Sumatra in search of a rhino for the imperial zoo. Buddhist texts date trade between India and Indonesia to the first century as well. In the West, Ptolemy of Alexandria seems to have been the first to indicate an awareness of the archipelago, although it was not until the return of the Venetian merchant Marco Polo from China in the thirteenth century that news of the Spice Islands drew the attention of European merchants.

During the first and second centuries, political units larger than the clan began to emerge, based on wet rice agriculture and coastal trade. These principalities grew in power owing to their strategic position as brokers of the growing commerce between India and China. The earliest known kingdoms were Taruma, centered near present-day Jakarta in the fifth and sixth centuries, and Srivijaya, on the coast of Sumatra. The "classical" era of Javanese culture began with the development in the seventh century of the rice-based kingdoms of central Java, the largest of which were Mataram (early eighth to ninth centuries; seventeenth and eighteenth centuries) and Majapahit (fourteenth to early sixteenth centuries). The religious orientation of these kingdoms alternated between Hindu and Buddhist, both faiths imported from India, and it was during this time that the great temple complexes of Java were erected: Borobudur (ninth century, Buddhist) and Prambanan (tenth century, Hindu). At its height in the fourteenth century, Majapahit claimed sovereignty over much of present-day Indonesia stretching from the southeast Asian mainland to New Guinea, although sovereignty in this case meant little more than control of interisland trade.

Beginning in the late thirteenth century, the influence of Islam began to be felt, as coastal states in western Sumatra and Malacca (on the south coast of the Malay

Buddhas meditate on a terrace of Borobudur, Java, a great temple complex of the eighth to ninth century.

Peninsula) converted to Islam, probably under the influence of their Muslim trade partners in south India. As Malacca grew in power, establishing links with merchants on the north coast of Java who embraced Islam, the control of trade began to shift from the hands of Majapahit. The growth of the spice trade with Europe also enhanced Malacca's position. Thus, by the sixteenth century, the center of political power had shifted from the Majapahit Empire in central Java to Malacca and the many mercantile city-states around the Java Sea.

This constellation of power shifted again when European trading ships arrived in the early sixteenth century. A Portuguese fleet captured Malacca in 1511. There began a century-long period of competition for control of the spice trade between the Portuguese in Malacca and the Muslim city-states such as Aceh on the northern tip of Sumatra and Makassar in Sulawesi. The Spanish moved south from the Philippines and the English also made an effort to "eliminate the middle man" in the spice trade, but it was the Dutch who succeeded.

Before we plunge into the 350 years of Dutch influence, it would be well to take stock of this long and extremely complex precolonial history. Indonesia has absorbed so many influences from so many sources that sorting them out has become a major industry among scholars of Southeast Asia. Certainly the Indian influence was most dominant in Java. There Hinduism and Buddhism were absorbed into the indigenous Javanese religion, Sanskrit was absorbed into the language, and the great Hindu epics, the *Mahabarata* and the *Ramayana*, became Java's national epics. The later adoption of Islam did not displace these influences but added another layer to the complex texture of Javanese culture.

The coastal states were more thoroughly Islamicized than the inland kingdoms, and the coastal peoples are to this day a major source of pressure for Indonesia to be declared an Islamic state. Much of the nation's political beliefs about the nature and power of the state date from this period, and it would be impossible to understand Indonesia's struggle to define itself as a nation without reference to the kingdoms of the past. It is the idea of Majapahit, not the Dutch East Indies, to which the national mythology turns when it tries to explain to itself how these thousands of islands became one country.

For the peoples of the Outer Islands, the influences of foreign commerce are much more limited to the artifacts of commerce itself. Chinese pottery, Indian beads and textiles, Portuguese indigo cloth, and Siamese brass drums are still stored away in attics under the thatched roofs of eastern Indonesia as family heirlooms and brideprice. But the culture and social structure of these peoples were still much as they had been before the first Chinese or Indian ships arrived. While doing research in eastern Indonesia I found no memory of Majapahit as a sovereign power, except for a mention here and there of "foreign trade" with Java in the distant past.

And what of the foreign traders themselves? Descendents of Indian and Arab merchants are still found scattered throughout the islands. Portuguese family names abound in Flores and Timor, and there remains to this day a rather charming Portuguese fishing village on the outskirts of Malacca, where they speak a unique dialect of sixteenth-century Portuguese and Malay and paint their doors with icons of the Virgin Mary. Many of the soldiers and sailors of the European mercantile powers had been desperately poor in their home countries, and they found in the Indies the opportunity for a much more prosperous life, even as farmers and fishermen. As for the Chinese, they are everywhere. The Dutch found them very useful: Where the local population proved difficult to conscript for plantation labor and mining, the Dutch turned to Chinese immigrants. They also found able business partners among the Chinese—a fact not lost on the Javanese elite, who in many respects simply replaced the Dutch after independence.

The Dutch East Indies

Dutch power in the Indies began with the establishment of Batavia (now Jakarta) in 1597. It was chosen as a base from which to challenge Portuguese power across the Straits in Malacca. For its first two hundred years, the Dutch presence was not that of a government but of a private trading company similar to that of the English in India.

The Company and Plantation Agriculture

The Dutch East Indies Company (VOC is its Dutch abbreviation) was established in 1602, arguably one of the first global corporations. Its strategy was a simple one: to control the lucrative trade between the Indies and Europe at its source. By a combination of treaties and force of arms, the Company began to assert control over the interisland trade network that had developed over the centuries. After clashing with the Javanese kingdom of Mataram, it established control of its base in West Java and succeeded in expelling the Portuguese from Malacca in 1641. In an effort to ensure Dutch monopoly of spices from the Moluccas (and to prevent lower prices due to oversupply), it allowed only Ambon to produce cloves, and it restricted production of nutmeg and mace to the Banda Islands. VOC troops were sent out to cut down spice trees outside the designated areas. Within fifty years, the Dutch had become the dominant commercial and maritime power in the Indies.

Initially, resistance to the Dutch centered around the coastal city-states, whose economic interests were most directly affected. Because they were mostly Islamic, the conflict took on religious dimensions as well. However, these states were scattered widely and had other enemies besides the Dutch, and they were not able to build a sustained force to dislodge the VOC. The VOC, by forging alliances with enemies of the Islamic city-states (including the Ambonese, the Bugis of Sulawesi, and the Hindu and Buddhist kingdom of Mataram in central Java), extended its control over a vast trade network and established fortresses in virtually all significant ports. For many years the Islamic traders who had formerly dominated the sea lanes continued to resist Dutch control but with limited success. Today they are remembered in Western history as the dreaded Malay pirates, the original bogeymen (erroneously derived from "Bugis," an ethnic group of southern Sulawesi). It might be more just to say that they were engaged in a naval form of guerrilla warfare.

It was not until the VOC turned its attention to plantation agriculture that the peoples of the interior regions felt the need to resist the Company's presence, but by then it was too late. The VOC set quotas for export crops and relied on the Javanese nobility to see that the quotas were met. Rice production, which fed the Javanese, declined in favor of coffee and sugar for European consumption, and the formerly prosperous Javanese began to feel the threat of food shortages. The VOC's policy was in essence a single-minded pursuit of trade; otherwise it interfered as little as possible with local governance. The Company sought to identify (or create) cooperative local rulers and then establish a monopoly on trade with them. If anything, the Dutch presence had the effect of centralizing power within the local kingdoms, whether for the sake of resisting or cooperating with them. It is important to remember that during the sixteenth and seventeenth centuries the concept of a "colony" was still emerging. The VOC was a trading company, not a government, and there was no clear distinction between terms of trade and political sovereignty. Not until 1798, when the VOC's bankruptcy left the Dutch government to take over its holdings, did the Indies become a colony in the modern sense.

The Dutch Government and the Culture System

At the time the Dutch government assumed control of the colonies, the Dutch were themselves embroiled in the political controversy that followed in the wake of

Young girls in Jakarta are still being trained in the highly stylized, graceful dances of Javanese tradition.

the French Revolution. The European debate over liberty and equality influenced the formation of Dutch colonial policy. Dutch liberals demanded that the colonies be governed by the same democratic principles that were being introduced in the Netherlands and proposed free trade and a system of land taxation. The colonial officials replied that such measures would eliminate Dutch profits from the colonies. The argument was quickly resolved: the liberals withdrew their demands. In a way, the colonials were right. Dutch monopoly of trade had been so successful that the once thriving regional commerce of the Indies had shriveled to a system of forced deliveries of export crops. The populace of the islands were so impoverished that there was no possibility of instituting the liberals' system of free trade and taxation.

To make a very long story very short, two major influences were at play here. First, the Dutch were faced with the classic colonial dilemma: how to extract as much profit as possible from the colonies without destroying the productivity of the colonized peoples. As any Dutch farmer knows, a healthy cow produces more milk. Second, it seemed both politically correct and expedient to reduce the power of the Javanese nobility. As the Netherlands struggled with the transformation from a monarchy dependent on a feudal nobility to the modern bureaucratic state, the colonies underwent a parallel process. After much fumbling about in search of alternatives, the Dutch officials instituted the Culture System. The traditional Javanese kingdoms and princedoms were broken down into administrative districts under a Dutch regent, and an effort was made to absorb the Javanese nobility into the colonial

Larry Tankersley

Traditional Torajan house on Sulawesi with upswept gable displays a stack of buffalo horns indicating the large number of buffalo sacrificed at a noble's costly funeral.

bureaucracy. At the same time, communal land was divided into privately owned plots, with the farmers devoting one fifth of their land to production of cash crops.

Unfortunately, the Dutch relied on the colonies to pay off a large national debt at home, which left the Javanese aristocracy in the position of trying to maintain their own customary affluence while meeting the financial demands of their Dutch overlords. The predictable result was widespread famine.

A Capitalist Economy

In the latter half of the nineteenth century, morally concerned Dutch liberals joined forces with Dutch capitalists to replace the Culture System with a more open economy. Capital investment was encouraged and a system of privately owned plantations developed. The owners were chiefly Dutch investors and Javanese nobles and merchants. The large and impoverished Javanese peasant population made an ideal source of labor for this purpose.

During this period the Dutch also began extending their power in the Outer Islands, mostly in response to the growing demand for raw materials for the Industrial Revolution then transforming Europe. To gain access to these resources they were again pitted against their old enemies, the Islamic coastal traders in Borneo and west Sumatra. By bribery, threat, and force of arms, they continued to extend their colonial bureaucracy into the interior of the Outer Islands up until World War II, when the arrival of the Japanese in 1942 brought everything to an abrupt halt.

The Legacy of Dutch Rule

What are we to conclude from this whirlwind tour of the Dutch colonial period? First, the reader may have noted that this account has been largely the story of Dutch interests versus the interests of local aristocrats and merchants. What of the ordinary people? For the villagers of Java and parts of Sumatra and the Moluccas, their plight was aptly summed up in a Malay proverb: "When elephants fight, the deer are trampled upon." It was mostly a history of oppression; by *whom* they were oppressed was of secondary importance. In the interior of the Outer Islands, the presence of the Dutch (or the Javanese, for that matter) was largely irrelevant until the beginning of the twentieth century.

Second, the strategy of the Dutch—to divide and conquer, and then to absorb the local nobility into the colonial bureaucracy—has been a model for much of Indonesian politics after independence. The present Suharto government has maintained its power by playing off ethnic and religious groups against one another, all in the name of national unity; and it has secured the loyalty of traditional leaders by assuring them a place in the highly centralized government bureaucracy.

Third, it can be seen that the single-minded focus on trade meant that the Dutch had relatively less cultural impact on the Indies than the English and Spanish had on their respective colonial empires. The Dutch used the Malay language for colonial administration and discouraged fraternization between the Dutch and the indigenous population. Until the latter part of the nineteenth century they also discouraged

Christian missionary activity on the grounds that it might disturb the local populace, which would in turn disturb trade.

Fourth, it should be recognized that if the Dutch did little to create a cultural unity among the diverse peoples of the archipelago, they nonetheless created a common system of law and administration that left in place the framework for the emergence of Indonesia as a modern state.

The Growth of Nationalism

At this point, most histories of Indonesia turn to the emergence of a nationalistic spirit in the early part of the twentieth century. I shall do the same, but I shall note one exception. Nationalism became meaningful for those social classes and in those areas of the archipelago most heavily influenced by the Dutch presence. For much of the Outer Islands, however, it was the very irrelevance of the idea of a "nation" that made national unity possible. Had they an idea of the nation state, it certainly wouldn't have included within its boundaries the hundreds of other peoples in the Dutch East Indies of whom they knew nothing more than could be gleaned from an occasional traveler's tale. For most of these indigenous peoples, although one ethnic group might come to dominate another, the idea of a transethnic unit of power simply didn't exist. Since such an idea didn't exist for them, they could neither embrace nor resist it.

The early decades of the twentieth century saw the development of a wide variety of popular organizations. The Dutch had begun to allow the children of nobility to receive a Western education, and in this way the Western ideals of democracy, human rights, and modern national government were eagerly absorbed by those groups among the populace of the Indies who were in the best position to put them to use. Budi Utomo (Noble Endeavor), the first nationalist organization, was founded by Dutch-educated Javanese nobility in 1908. Their chief practical goal was the establishment of a national school system. Shortly thereafter a more broad-based organization with its greatest strength in the merchant class was formed, the Sarekat Islam (Islamic Union). Inspired by the success of the Russian revolution, a faction of the Sarekat Islam broke away to form the Indonesian Communist Party (PKI) in 1920. Labor unions were also formed and carried out a series of strikes during this period. In 1929, the National Party of Indonesia issued a call for independence and was immediately suppressed. Its leaders were exiled to the Outer Islands, among them the young engineer Sukarno.

The strategies of these nationalist groups varied from cooperative evolution toward independence, to noncooperation in the style of Mahatma Gandhi of India, to armed struggle. The Dutch responded predictably by seeking to placate the cooperative factions and to suppress the rest. An uneasy standoff prevailed during the global depression of the 1930s. Then World War II broke out. The Netherlands was occupied by Germany in 1940, and the Japanese invaded the Dutch East Indies in 1942.

Independence

The Japanese were at first greeted as liberators by the Indonesians. Under the Greater East Asia Co-prosperity Sphere promised by the invaders, the Japanese were to be big brothers leading the colonized peoples of Southeast Asia into freedom. In reality, of course, the Japanese wanted what everyone else had wanted over the centuries: natural resources and cheap labor. Famine, rape, forced labor, and summary execution were daily realities, and yet many Indonesians cooperated with the Japanese, not only for fear of their lives but in the hope that somehow cooperation would aid them in achieving their independence.

They were right. As defeat seemed inevitable, the Japanese armed and trained an Indonesian militia, which, along with remnants of indigenous troops who had served in the Dutch colonial army, formed the core of the revolutionary force that would repel the Dutch when they sought to return to their colony. Hiroshima was bombed on August 9, 1945, the Japanese surrendered on August 15, and on August 17 Sukarno, who had worked closely with the Japanese to prepare for the event, proclaimed independence. A constitution was drawn up, which provided for a parliamentary style of government, reserving broad but "not unlimited" powers to the president. After a period of revolution during which the Dutch fought to reinstate their control, the Netherlands finally recognized Indonesia's independence on December 29, 1949.

During the first decade of independence under President Sukarno, Indonesia struggled to implement a West European-style parliamentary democracy. Dozens of new parties and political factions were formed based on regional, ethnic, ideological, and religious affinities. The tenuous bonds of national identity were repeatedly tested, not only by a chaotic political climate but by outright rebellion and attempts at secession in Sumatra, Sulawesi, and the Moluccas. Islamic guerrilla movements in Java, Aceh, and South Sulawesi attempted to replace the secular European model of government with an Islamic state. These conflicts were eventually resolved only by military force, which served further to entrench the power of the Army as the enforcer of national unity.

Despairing of the ability of liberal democracy to bring order to this vast and diverse nation, President Sukarno "rationalized" political parties, declared a return to the 1945 Constitution, and dubbed the new system with an exquisite oxymoron: "Guided Democracy." However, centralized control of the political economy proved impossible without the infrastructure to support it. Foreign investment withdrew, the economy stagnated, and inflation skyrocketed. Even though many Indonesians remember this as the worst period since the Japanese occupation, Sukarno's popularity remained high. He was able with some justification to attribute Indonesia's woes to the power of foreign capital and political subversion. The United States saw Sukarno's close relations with China and the Soviet Union as a threat and gave covert aid to secessionists—covert, that is, until a U.S. spy plane was shot down over Sulawesi in 1962 while delivering arms to rebels there.

To retain power, Sukarno had to juggle the interests of the three most powerful factions in the country: the Army, Muslim proponents of an Islamic state, and the Communists, who had developed effective grassroots organizations and whose party, the PKI, had grown to be the largest Communist party outside the Soviet bloc. In an attempt to unify (or at least pacify) these forces, Sukarno articulated a political philosophy he called NASAKOM, which is the Indonesian acronym for nationalism, religion, and socialism.

It didn't work. In September 1965 there was an attempted coup. The real actors behind the coup are still the subject of much controversy, but it was blamed on the Communists. After a number of the Army's top generals were assassinated, Colonel Suharto of the Jakarta security forces took the lead in organizing a campaign to wipe out the Communists and their supporters. Hundreds of thousands were killed in the reign of terror that followed. It left a residue of fear and guilt that has haunted Indonesian political life up to the present. In March 1966 Sukarno ceded power to Suharto, and the Sukarno era came to its end.

The New Order

To mark a fundamental break with the Sukarno era, Suharto and his Army proclaimed an *Orde Baru*, a "new order." The "new" part of the name was a shift toward free market capitalism; the military would provide the "order." Suharto assigned economic planning to a group of mostly American-educated economists and technocrats. A series of five-year plans was instituted, and national economic development became the goal toward which all other interests were to be sacrificed. The military insured a strike-free, pro-capital environment, while government officials (many drawn from the military as well) and their families became the brokers of foreign investment. Sale of natural resources, especially oil, provided the funds needed for investment in infrastructure and development of industry. A network of roads, schools, hospitals, and telecommunications began to spread from Java through the Outer Islands. By the end of the 1980s, the nation had achieved self-sufficiency in rice production, an average life expectancy of sixty-two, a population growth rate reduced from 3 to 2 percent, a literacy rate of 80 percent, and a sustained economic growth rate of about 7 percent annually. It would seem that Indonesia's rich potential was finally beginning to be realized.

Tension and Conflict

However—and there is a long list of "howevers"—these achievements came at a price. Tensions began to build between the Outer Islands (which provided most of the natural resources) and Java (which, as the manufacturing center, received most of the benefits). To many, it seemed that the Javanese upper class had simply replaced the Dutch as colonizers, especially in areas where tribal lands were expropriated for mining and timber interests and where large numbers of Javanese had been resettled (the transmigration program) to relieve the population pressure on Java. There was a strong feeling that the Javanese looked down upon Outer Islanders as racially inferior. In Aceh and Irian Jaya, separatist groups continue to operate despite often brutal attempts by the military to suppress them. In January 1997 a state of ethnic warfare broke out between Dayaks of Kalimantan and trans-migrants from Madura in which nearly a thousand people are believed to have been killed.

Perhaps the accusation of being neocolonial is most accurately applied in the case of East Timor. This former Portuguese colony was invaded by Indonesia in December 1975 (with the blessing of U.S. Secretary of State Henry Kissinger and President Gerald Ford and the use of American-made weapons). After the 1974 coup in Portugal when the dictator Antonio de Oliveira Salazar was overthrown, Portugal began a rather hasty process of decolonization in its African and Southeast Asian colonies. In East Timor this process resulted in a brief civil war. Nervous at the prospect of a socialist group coming to power, Indonesia moved in on the pretext that it had been invited to intervene by pro-integrationists in East Timor. In the warfare and famine that followed, nearly a third of the indigenous population are thought to have died. Resistance continues and, more than twenty years later, East Timor still lives under military occupation. Perhaps not coincidentally, major oil reserves were discovered off the Timor coast in the early 1970s.

On Java itself, conflict has arisen over expropriation of agricultural land for industry, housing, and even golf courses (Suharto is an avid golfer). In the 1990s, attempts to establish independent labor unions and strikes by workers to seek a liv-ing wage have been suppressed by the military. The rape and murder of Marsinah, a labor activist who led a strike at a watch factory in East Java, has become a sym-bol of the human sacrifice exacted by Indonesia's industrialization.

Conflict also exists between the Chinese and indigenous populations. Just as they had been partners to the Dutch, Chinese are now prominent among the busi-ness associates of the ruling class. Among this group of Indonesian Chinese are sev-eral of the richest individuals in the world. Anti-Chinese riots have broken out spo-radically throughout the period of the New Order (as they had in Dutch times as well). Still more tensions are apparent between practicing Muslims and secularists, Muslims and Christians, Catholics and Protestants, merchants and peasants, and of course, rich and poor. What has thus far kept all these cracks in the social landscape from tearing the country apart is that they do not coalesce along a major fault line; conflicting interests are held in check by common interests. And when things get out of hand, the military is on the spot. Their willingness to shoot unarmed protesters, combined with the residue of fear from 1965, have so far been enough to keep a cap on the unrest.

Unity and Pancasila

In order to keep these divisive tendencies in check, political life is highly regu-lated by the government: three parties are allowed to operate, but Golkar, the offi-cial government party, is always the winner in any election. The other two parties are the Indonesian Democratic Party (PDI), which consists of liberal democrats, including many Christians, and the United Development Party (PPP), a moderate

Soldiers escort the shield of the Pancasila ("Five Pillars") in an Independence Day parade in Kupang, Timor.

Islamic party. Campaigning is restricted, the press is censored, and criticising the president is punishable by imprisonment. Likewise only one, government-controlled labor union is allowed to operate freely. Those who seriously challenge the Suharto government are liable to charges of subversion, which carries a maximum penalty of death. Subversion trials are currently underway of Mokhtar Pakpahan, a Sumatran labor leader, and members of the banned People's Democratic Party (a recently formed coalition of student and labor activists). No one has ever been acquitted of subversion.

Further to promote unity, all parties and indeed all social and religious organizations are required to subscribe to the *Pancasila* ("Five Pillars") as their sole ideological foundation. The "pillars" are 1) belief in the one supreme God 2) just and civilized humanity 3) the unity of Indonesia 4) sovereignty of the people guided by inner wisdom in the unanimity arising out of deliberations among representatives, and 5) social justice for the whole people of Indonesia. Taken by themselves, these are all laudable values; but many think that the state ideology has been used by the government as an all-purpose political homogenizer. If one objects that current political restrictions are undemocratic, the official reply will be, "Ah, but you are trying to import a foreign model of liberal democracy. We have a Pancasila democracy."

Rising Discontent

Suharto has remained in power since 1965, running for reelection as the sole candidate every five years. At seventy-six, he showed no sign of stepping aside in the 1997 elections, nor are any clear successors on the horizon. But pressure for change is building. Riots on July 27, 1996, in Jakarta followed the forcible takeover of the Indonesian Democratic Party headquarters by the military because of the party's support for Megawati Sukarnoputri, former President Sukarno's daughter, as a candidate for the presidency. These events came as the climax to a long season of unrest in many parts of the country. Students were killed in April of that year in Ujung Pandang (South Sulawesi) when their campus was raided by troops in retaliation for demonstrations they had held objecting to a sudden increase in public transportation fares. A succession of labor actions, illegal under Indonesia's pro-investor labor laws, had disrupted cities from Medan to Surabaya. Riots broke out in Irian Jaya when the body of a separatist leader, who had died in a prison in Jakarta under mysterious circumstances, was brought home for burial. Other demonstrations on that island protested the expropriation and exploitation of tribal lands on behalf of the American mining giant Freeport-McMoRan. Several villagers had also been murdered by troops acting on Freeport's behalf. In June 1996 demonstrations against Indonesian military occupation broke out once again in Baucau, the second largest city in East Timor.

When it seemed that these widespread and widely varied expressions of discontent with President Suharto's New Order were finding an effective political channel in the Indonesian Democratic Party and its gentle leader, Megawati, the Suharto government engineered a spurious party congress to unseat Megawati and replace her with a puppet leadership. Party loyalists then refused to give up the party headquarters in Jakarta to the usurpers. Sympathizers gathered daily and formed a human wall around the building. An open microphone gave opportunity for pro-democracy activists to give expression to a host of grievances normally kept quiet by Indonesia's tightly controlled press. They spoke of rampant corruption in the government bureaucracy and judiciary, protested the domination of the economy by Suharto's rapaciously greedy children, and condemned the government's iron-fisted control of political expression and its use of the military to protect its political and economic interests.

Perhaps fearing a Philippine-style People's Power movement, the government ordered the expulsion of PDI loyalists. Early on the morning of July 27, 1996, a group of thugs (whom many believe to have been troops in civilian clothing) led an attack that resulted in an unknown number of deaths and more than two hundred arrests. In response to this attack, thousands rioted in central Jakarta, burning a number of banks, businesses, and government buildings and effectively shutting down the center of the capital. Since these events, the Suharto government has reacted true to character by rounding up student, labor, and pro-democracy activists and trying to portray them as members of a Communist conspiracy.

The political grapevine says that the government engineered a state of chaos in the PDI under the code name Operation Red Dragon. Red is the color of the PDI. As the story goes, next in line was Operation Green Dragon. Green, of course, is the color of the other opposition party, the largely Islamic PPP. Here the strategy was to incite anti-Christian riots in small cities in Java that could easily be controlled by the military. Such riots would portray the leadership of Muslim groups as dangerous fanatics, thus driving all right-thinking moderates into the arms of Golkar (the reigning government party) and the Army. Whether this scenario is close to the truth will probably not be known until after the close of the New Order. One can expect no Watergate-style reporting from Indonesia's closely watched press. The fact remains that more than two hundred churches were burned in Java in recent years.

As 1997 drew to a close, the situation in Indonesia looked bleaker than it has for many years: forest fires, burning in Kalimantan and Sumatra since May, left a pall of smoke over much of Southeast Asia that grew to half the size of the continental United States. The same prolonged drought that exacerbated the fires led to famine in many rural areas. More than five hundred people were known to have died of starvation in Irian Jaya, and villagers in Java were reduced to selling their possessions just to buy water for drinking and cooking. Beginning in August, the rupiah went into a free fall along with other Asian currencies that led to a 30 percent devaluation against the dollar. Stock markets plunged and a $23 billion rescue package was put together with the International Monetary Fund. As a result of the economic crisis, thousands are in danger of losing their jobs just as IMF-mandated austerity measures reduce government subsidies and prices of staple goods begin to rise. The possibility of widespread unrest hangs over the country like an impending storm.

It would be unfair and inaccurate to let this catalog of crises completely dominate our picture of Indonesia. Economic growth continues apace, and many have felt its benefits. Indonesia is already a major economic power in Southeast Asia and seems poised to take a role in international affairs more in keeping with its position as the world's fourth largest nation. No one would want to return to the time of chaos before 1965. Perhaps the reflections of a friend from Timor are a good summary of the mood of the country: "We are grateful for the accomplishments of the Suharto era. But along with development has come so much greed and corruption and oppression that, well, we're just about nauseated by it."

An ancient Javanese belief holds that the end of a century will also mark the end of a kingdom. Indonesians are waiting and watching.

A Morning with the *Jakarta Post*

There is nothing like a look at the local newspaper to give you a sense of what's going on in a country. One morning in Yogyakarta I have a break from teaching, and I sit down with a strong cup of coffee and the day's paper: There's the usual wire service stuff. Israel and the PLO reach yet another agreement (the

Middle East is of special interest to the world's largest Muslim population, or at least it is supposed to be). At least one business story features prominently, since most of the readers of an English-language daily in a non-English-speaking country will be expatriate business people. Today it's the projected merger of two Canadian mining companies for the purpose of exploiting the gold reserves of Kalimantan (an estimated 57 million ounces, let's see, at $350 an ounce . . .). The real paydirt in the story, however, is tucked away toward the end: which of the companies is aligned with which of Suharto's children. The merger proposal winds up looking like a way to resolve a fight among presidential siblings. I wonder how the Canadian shareholders would feel about that. [This turned out to be the Bre-X scandal, a hoax because there was no gold.]

Then there's the inevitable headline that is completely indecipherable to an outsider. "Yellow Policy Criticized." What could this mean? Does it refer to censorship of yellow journalism? No, that's an American idiom, if not an exclusively American phenomenon. Could it be that the government has started regulating the primary colors? It tries to regulate everything else. As it turns out, yes. The government of central Java has declared that all public signs, including the inevitable pillars marking the gateway to a village, are to be painted yellow. What the reader must know is that the three legal political parties in Indonesia are color-coded. The Islamic Development Party is green, the liberal Indonesian Democratic Party is red, and Golkar, the ruling government party is (you guessed it) yellow.

But the story that makes me put the paper down and stare at the wall for a while comes from the "curiosities" section tucked away in the lower right-hand corner of the front page. "Flat Nose Proves Deadly Frustrating." A man has been arrested for knifing his girlfriend to death after he learned she had squandered the money he gave her for a nose job. The idea was to make her flat Javanese nose more like a straight Western nose. You might say she died for beauty. But whose idea of beauty was it, anyway, and how did this crazy man get that idea into his head? I held the answer in my hands: turn the pages of any newspaper or magazine here in Indonesia and you'll find plenty of straight noses selling cars, clothing, and cigarettes. But I didn't want to look at them just then.

Chapter 2

The Global Sweatshop

Check the labels on your clothes. Where were they made? Even those labeled "Made in the U.S." or "Made in Canada" may have been only finished and packaged there. Increasingly, North Americans are clothed by workers in the developing countries, where labor is cheap and governments vie to create "a climate favorable to investment." Once only discount chains sold cheap clothing made in Hong Kong or Taiwan. Now, designer brands have also followed the labor market overseas in what has come to be called the Global Sweatshop. Clothing by Ralph Lauren, Liz Claiborne, and Perry Ellis and shoes by Nike, Reebok, and Adidas are manufactured by subcontractors in Indonesia.

How cheap is labor in Indonesia? The official minimum wage amounts to about $2.50 a day—not enough to meet the basic daily needs of one adult, by the government's own calculations. Wages are so low that the labor cost of sneakers that sell for $75 to $100 in the United States is only about $1.75. Many workers do not even receive minimum wage; in fact it is often the chief demand over which they go on strike.

A strike is risky business in this "climate favorable to investment." Under the doctrine of the "dual function" of the military, the Indonesian Army is called upon to promote economic development as well as defend the nation from external aggression. This role has often included forcibly putting down labor unrest when factory management called for military assistance. Although U.S. pressure brought about a presidential order repealing this practice in 1994, the repeal has had limited effect.

The Indonesian government has also sought to prevent labor from organizing freely by mandating a single national labor union, the All-Indonesia Labor Union

(SPSI). Not surprisingly, the head of this union is not a worker but a well-connected owner of a group of clothing factories. Attempts to form independent unions are routinely quashed. Here is a classic sequence of events: On July 29, 1993, the Indonesian government prevented an independent trade union, the Prosperous Workers' Union of Indonesia (SBSI), from holding its first national congress. The police said they were closing down the meeting because the organizers did not have a permit. Although they had requested a permit, the police had refused to grant them one on the grounds that they needed recommendations from the Ministries of Manpower and Home Affairs. The recommendations were not forthcoming because, according to the Manpower Ministry, the SBSI was not a true labor union. If it had been, it would have upheld the 1973 Declaration of Workers, recognizing the one single union (the government's own SPSI) as a force for national unity and the best guarantor of workers' welfare. After these polite explanations, the organizers were arrested. Their leader, Mukhtar Pakpahan, is currently on trial for his life.

A twenty-three-year-old worker in a watch factory named Marsinah has become the symbol of the plight of Indonesian labor. On May 3–4, 1993, Marsinah joined her fellow workers at P. T. Catur Putra Surya, in the district of Sidoarjo, East Java, in a two day sit-down strike. They demanded compliance with the minimum-wage law, the dissolution of the factory unit of SPSI (the government-sponsored union), and ten other items. By noon on the first day, eighteen workers had been taken to the sub-district military headquarters, interrogated, and accused of inciting the strike. Two days later, when Marsinah (who had been one of the strike leaders) went to visit her jailed comrades, she was told they had already been released. Three days later, on May 8, her body was found two hundred kilometers (160 miles) from the factory in a hut by a rice paddy. An autopsy found evidence that Marsinah died as a result of injuries inflicted during torture. Lesions on her neck and both wrists indicated she had been severely beaten and had suffered internal hemorrhaging, her pelvic bones were broken, and she had been raped with a sharp object, fifteen to twenty centimeters (six to eight inches) in diameter. The killing generated a public outcry throughout Indonesia. Presumably the killers thought her fate would serve as a warning to other labor activists. At the time of her death, Marsinah had been earning the equivalent of eighty cents a day.

Restrictions on organizing are not merely to keep wages down in order to attract and retain foreign investors. The government also remembers the role of labor in the beginnings of resistance to the Dutch and in the fall of the Sukarno government. There is a fear that labor will join with progressive students in a broader pro-democracy movement—as in fact it did in massive demonstrations in Medan in 1994 and Surabaya in 1996. Given the anticommunist phobia of the New Order, any alliance between students and workers must seem reminiscent of Lenin's strategies. More to the point, however, is the fact that when student sympathies swing toward labor, it is an early indicator of discontent among the middle class, since most university students are from middle-income families. And it just goes against the totalitarian temper of the Suharto government to allow anyone at all to organize or gather in public without government control.

"But why are they willing to work in these factories if conditions are so bad?" That is a reasonable question. Perhaps the story of one worker can give us some insight into what motivates the thousands of young women who sew our clothes and our shoes. The following account is adapted from the field notes of Peter Hancock, an Australian scholar doing research on factory workers in Sunda, West Java.

SUMI'S SACRIFICE

Sumi, age seventeen, is the oldest daughter in a very poor rural family. Her parents, three sisters, and one brother live in a rented house in a mountain village. Sumi travels daily to the lowlands, where she has worked in a shoe factory called Kukje for three years. Sumi left school when she was fourteen because it was too expensive and her father's meager wage could not afford her fees and travel costs to and from school. Sumi's father also works in a factory and has done so for fifteen years. However, he works as a security guard for only Rp. 123,000 (US$38) a month.

Since she started work Sumi has been the main income earner in her family. Their small house is sparsely furnished and extremely overcrowded. The father's income is used to buy food and other daily necessities. Sumi's income is used for clothing, health care, and other costs, especially to help her younger sisters finish school. Sumi says she will not marry or leave the factory until her sisters have left high school, which will be another twelve years. She says she hates the factory work, but without her income her family would be almost destitute. Sumi has no dreams for her own future; she knows that without an education she has no hope.

Many Indonesian women work long hours for low pay sewing clothes in foreign-owned factories.

She says that she will sacrifice her future for her sisters to have an education. One of them wants to be an air hostess, which means she must complete senior high school. Sumi is paying for all her school costs and Sumi hopes her sister will be successful. Sumi's dreams of the future are in fact her sisters' dreams.

Sumi works in the stitching section of a Nike factory. She must work long hours, six and sometimes seven days a week. Because she is a reliable and honest worker she is required for all the overtime available. Normally she works fifty-five hours a week for a monthly wage of Rp. 230,000 (US$71). I went shopping with Sumi on a pay day; the only luxury item she bought for herself was a bar of soap, the rest she keeps for her family's needs. Sumi never complains; if a family member becomes ill, Sumi has to pay for doctor's fees and medicines. If the family runs out of food, Sumi pays, and in emergencies and festivals her wages are crucial.

Sumi is paid the legal minimum wage and gets a few benefits such as sick leave and correct overtime pay. However, she must work very long hours to increase her wages to the extent that they can cover family expenses. Only seventeen, she is proud to be supporting her family, and she is very close to them. They are very cohesive as a family despite living in a small, two-room bamboo house. They have an old black-and-white TV, but there are no beds. Rice is the staple diet. The cooking, cleaning, toilet, and bathroom facilities are all contained in one small outdoor compound shared by five other families. At first Sumi was embarrassed about her living conditions and would not let me see them until she came to know me better.

Sumi's family have a strong belief in Islam and in Allah. Every day when Sumi leaves for work and again when she returns she says loudly and proudly to her family, "May Allah be with you," to which a chorus of voices replies, "And with you." If it were not for her family's desperate position she would leave the factory. She told me she thinks about it every day. She wants to leave and find a husband, because at eighteen most of her village friends will be married. But she cannot leave the factory; she has no choice.

Analysis: Understanding Sumi's Situation

If we look more carefully at Sumi's situation, the first thing to note is that Sumi is relatively better off than many of her fellow workers. She earns the minimum wage and is allowed sick leave. Many other workers find that if they are sick or injured on the job, they are immediately fired. With so large a labor pool they are easily replaced. A high rate of turnover among workers has several advantages to management: long-term workers are more likely to agitate for better pay and working conditions, and the widespread practice of demanding kickbacks for granting someone employment means that the more often new workers are hired, the more kickbacks the managers receive.

Another favorable condition for Sumi is that she is able to live at home rather than in a factory barracks, where workers may sleep three and four to a bed. Also there are no reports of her maltreatment by factory management. Labor-rights monitors in other places have documented many cases of sexual harassment, verbal abuse, slapping, and even strip searches to determine whether women are truly eligible for menstrual rest privileges. Again, Sumi's situation seems to be better than many.

Sumi also has the satisfaction of being able to make a net contribution to the family income. Many workers cannot do so. With the minimum wage set at less than the daily requirement to support a single adult, the families of these workers are effectively subsidizing the factories. They accept this strange situation for three reasons. First, even though families must often send food from home, pay transportation costs, or buy clothing for their working children, the income from the factory job reduces the amount the family would otherwise need in order to support an unemployed child at home. Second, there is always the hope for a raise or a promotion or that the current job will lead to a better one. And finally, the social status of a factory worker in Indonesia is usually higher than that of an agricultural worker, even though the net benefits may actually be lower. The desire to be "modern" and not "backward" is a powerful social force. In any event, agriculture is in decline in Java as industrialization and urban expansion reduce the amount of land under cultivation, and population density has reduced the average amount of land per family to less than half a hectare (about one acre). Since Sumi's family is landless, she may not have the option of agricultural work.

In Sumi's case, it seems clear that family solidarity is her chief motive in holding her job. She is justifiably proud that she makes such a significant contribution to the family income. (We do not learn how her father feels, knowing that his seventeen-year-old daughter earns almost twice what he does. His situation is not unusual, however. More than 80 percent of factory workers in the garment and athletic shoe industries are women, apparently because women are considered more dextrous and more submissive to male management.) It is likely that despite the daily drudgery of her life, Sumi takes great satisfaction in knowing that she is successfully fulfilling her role as a dutiful daughter and elder sister. It is entirely normal in Indonesia that an individual's desires should be set aside for the sake of the family or community. Such self-sacrifice is also apparent in the fact that despite the family's poverty, Sumi's wages are sometimes used for the festive celebrations that are such an important part of life in an Indonesian community. Utilitarian North Americans may question this expenditure, but if one values self-respect and religious obligation as highly as material possessions, not to observe important community and religious festivals (usually involving special foods and small gifts) would be deeply humiliating.

The road not taken in Sumi's life is education. Here too she is not alone. Only 60 percent of Indonesians age thirteen to fifteen attend school. Although the opportunity for an elementary education is now nearly universal, there is a high drop-out

In modern Indonesia, elementary school is mandatory for both boys and girls, but the cost of school fees, books, uniforms, and travel is a serious problem for many families.

rate in the shift to junior high and high school. As with Sumi's family, the cost of having a child in school presents a double burden on poor families: not only do they have to pay for books, school uniforms, tuition, and transportation to and from school, they also lose the income they would receive if the child were working. (The minimum age for employment in Indonesia is thirteen.) For the farm population there is the added liability that while the child is in school, he or she is not available to learn the skills of the parents—such as farming, animal care, sewing, and weaving. The content of the public school curriculum still bears the marks of the Dutch colonial system, which was designed to produce secretarial and administrative workers for the colonial bureaucracy, not to provide the skills needed for agriculture, a trade, or other employment. It is hard to argue with a farmer who decides not to send his child to school. As one farmer told me about his son, an unemployed high school graduate, "They ruined him for farming—he thinks he's too good for it now—but they didn't teach him how to do anything else."

Nonetheless, education is widely believed to be the key to advancing one's economic status over the long term. The strategy of many families is to sacrifice one child for the sake of the others, which seems to be what happened in Sumi's case. Her income provides just enough economic boost to enable her younger siblings to attend school. If all goes well, there are no serious illnesses, and Sumi doesn't marry or lose her job, perhaps there will be enough money for her siblings to finish school and find better jobs than she has.

What of Sumi's future? Perhaps in fifteen years she will be on her way to becoming a matriarch. Her brother and sisters will owe her a debt of gratitude, and

perhaps they will repay her with respect and economic security. But it is just as likely that she will find herself at middle age worn out from factory work, unmarried, her siblings scattered to wherever the search for work has taken them, leaving her to care for aging parents.

You needn't try to put yourself in Sumi's shoes (she probably wears flip-flops, anyway). But imagine for a moment that she made *your* shoes. How do they feel?

Everyone works to help support the family; sometimes even children take care of younger children instead of going to school.

Interpretation: A "Glocal" Issue

The Indonesian language is rife with newly created words. A Javanese friend who works for the World Council of Churches introduced me to this neologism: *glocal*, meaning something that has both global and local implications. The labor issues just reflected upon are as global as the World Bank and as local as the shoes on your feet. The contents of your home are probably a veritable museum of international trade. Perhaps the larger appliances, furniture, and a few odds and ends were made in the United States or Canada, but most of your electronic goods, small appliances, shoes, and clothing probably come from China, Haiti, Mexico, Korea, Japan, and maybe even from Indonesia. People like Sumi and Marsinah made them for you, often under conditions that would be prohibited by law if they occurred in your country. If you are an American or Canadian factory worker, this situation may have caused you to lose your job or to experience a decline in wages and living conditions. But as a consumer, you have most certainly benefited in the form of lower prices and greater choices. If you own stock in multinational corporations or have interest in a pension fund, you have benefited even more.

That North Americans are morally implicated in the inequities of the global economy is clear; whether we are morally culpable is a different question. After all, few of us had any direct role in making the decisions that have shaped the current world economy. The problem is that hardly anyone at all will admit to responsibility. Corporate executives claim they are merely responding to "market forces" and fulfilling their fiduciary responsibility to investors to maximize profit. What are "market forces" anyway? Are they like the tides or the jet stream? Or are they like Paul's "powers of the air," mysterious elemental spirits that can only be divined by their priests, the CEOs of multinational corporations? In his classic eighteenth-century statement of capitalist faith, *The Wealth of Nations*, Adam Smith referred to these mysterious powers as the "unseen hand" that guides the behavior of a multitude of self-seeking individuals toward the greater good. Individuals are thereby absolved of moral deliberation because the God of the Unseen Hand is the only moral agent. Indeed, the assigned role of human agents, both producers and consumers, is precisely to be amoral in the pursuit of their own self-interest. Self-interest provides the engine of greed that is magically transformed by competition into the greater good. As Paul puts it (ironically, in his case), "Let sin increase that grace might abound." But there is no irony here, only contradiction. This is the moral fiction by which capitalist faith sustains itself.

But aren't Indonesian workers better off for having the jobs provided by multinationals? That is difficult to answer. Measured in gross domestic product, it is true that there has been a dramatic rise under Suharto's New Order—from $70 per capita in 1967 to $1,000 in 1994. Life expectancy has also risen dramatically—from forty-one in 1965 to sixty-three in 1994—while infant mortality and illiteracy rates have plummeted. At the same time, however, Indonesia's foreign debt has climbed to one of the largest in the developing world: more than $100 billion. The borrowed money was used in part to build the infrastructure required by modern industry: roads, telecommunications, and facilities for water and electricity. Certainly the general population has experienced some benefit from these facilities as well. Yet the need for foreign exchange to service the debt forces the economy to concentrate on exports more than on serving local needs. All this outside money is also a magnet for corruption. Foreign investment, loans, and even aid wind up strengthening the Indonesian ruling class. They are able to divert public funds to their private benefit, leaving the people with a huge debt to pay. In a vicious circle, this debt is then used to justify low wages and repressive labor conditions for the sake of attracting more foreign investment.

Furthermore, a higher gross domestic product does not automatically ensure a higher per capita income. The benefits of increased productivity have gone mostly to investors rather than to workers, leaving Indonesians with the lowest per capita income in Southeast Asia, despite their country's remarkable economic growth. In this Indonesian workers are but one example of what has happened worldwide with the growth of a global economy. In the past thirty years, U.S. workers have experienced a real decline in wages while the gap between rich and poor has increased dramatically. In 1960 worldwide the top 20 percent of the population earned thirty times what the bottom 20 percent earned. Today, the top 20 percent earns sixty-one times more. The disparity is even greater if we compare Sumi's earnings with those of others on the Nike payroll. The basketball star Michael Jordan, whose only labor is to pose for commercials, earns more annually from Nike than *all Indonesian Nike factory workers combined.*

The current situation, in which companies are allowed to pay less than the minimum daily wage required for survival, is in effect more profitable than slavery. If factories owned slaves, they would have to support them at a subsistence level. As it is now, they can rely on the families of their workers to subsidize their industry. Maybe this practice seems acceptable because there's no personal ownership involved; we can't say, "Siti is owned by Bob." But the mass of landless laborers are coerced by poverty just as surely as slaves were coerced by whips.

Subcontractors are not entirely to blame for this situation: international labor monitors have reported that bidding for athletic shoe contracts is so competitive that the low wages are virtually dictated by the shoe companies. Could Nike afford to pay more? Well, its profits in 1996 were $673 million, and the company's founder, Philip Knight, has a reported personal fortune of $5 billion.

So, to return to the question of whether Indonesian workers are better off, the answer is mixed. They are a little better off financially, but they have not been nearly as well rewarded as factory owners, the politically powerful, and foreign investors. At the same time, many Indonesians have told me that they feel less secure than in the days of an agrarian economy; and they are less free because the growth of an export economy has entrenched the power of the ruling class and encouraged repression. This is true even in the Outer Islands, where there have been massive expropriations of traditional tribal lands for the sake of acquiring raw materials for industry and export (see chapter 3, "The Dilemmas of Development").

To answer the question whether North Americans are morally to blame for this state of affairs, I would say that the corporate decision makers certainly are; but if you are not among that select group of "ruling elite," your part in the problem is only indirect. You didn't create this situation knowingly, although your behavior as a consumer is what makes it all possible: you buy the clothes and the shoes. So let's put it this way: if you were standing on someone's hand, wouldn't you want to know about it, so you could move your foot? By way of conclusion, I want to offer a few suggestions as to how you can "move your foot."

Action

The global economy will not be reformed in a day, and in the meantime we will be morally compromised every time we shop. We do not control the means of production for the products we use in our daily lives, so we cannot by ourselves ensure that they will be made under conditions that are fair to the workers. We have basically three options: legislation, persuasion, and change in our patterns of buying and consumption. These methods have been used with some success in protecting endangered species and the environment; it is now time to use them to protect people as well.

The most direct action you can take is to boycott products you have reason to believe were made under sweatshop conditions. Find out where products were made, and wherever possible, buy locally made products or products you have reason to believe were made under conditions that are fair to the workers. Your local co-op is a good place to start, as many co-ops screen their merchandise for "fair exchange" practices.

When you have no other choice, either go without or buy the product but express your unhappiness at being implicated in immoral business practices. Express your concern to the management of the stores where you shop. Discuss these issues in local schools and with coaches and local athletic teams. Write to Nike and other manufacturers encouraging them to pay a fair wage. Finally, let your legislators know how you feel. U.S. and Canadian trade policies are almost entirely directed at advancing the interests of their national corporations, to the detriment of workers both here and abroad. Concerned consumers need to establish the principle that any company that cannot afford to pay a living wage to its workers is not a viable company.

The structure of the global economy will only change when consumers and workers together make life so unpleasant for multinational predators that they are forced to change. Encouraged by support from abroad, 10,000 Nike workers went on strike in Jakarta in April 1997. They won an increase in their daily wage from $2.26 to $2.46. Perhaps justice will only be gained in this way, twenty cents at a time. We can take encouragement from the closing words of a letter from jail by a group of Indonesian labor organizers. On the very day of the Nike strike, a young woman in their group, Dita Sari, was sentenced to six years in prison. They quote from the Koran: "O people of faith! May you always uphold what is right, for God is the witness of the just."

Bachelors of Unemployment

Sumi is making great sacrifices so that her younger brother and sisters can attend school. What happens when they graduate? The following report is adapted from a case study first published in *Case Studies in Social Development* (1996), edited by Rev. M. S. E. Simorangkir.

The *Sipardame* congregation is located near a Christian university in the town of Buhasingari in North Sumatra. A large percentage of worshipers are students. There are so many, in fact, that three services are required every Sunday. The 8:00

A.M. service has about 800 to 950 worshipers, the 10:00 A.M. service 600 to 700, and the evening service at 7:00 P.M. 400 to 450. The students, from a wide variety of Protestant denominations, are active in choirs, vocal groups, and the church youth group.

One evening after youth group, the pastor noticed that Marmulia, one of the students, seemed unusually quiet. He asked her what was wrong.

"I have a lot of problems on my mind, Pastor," she answered.

"May I ask what is troubling you?"

Marmulia answered unashamedly in front of her friends, "I graduated from the Faculty of Mathematics and Natural Sciences more than two years ago, but I still have no work. I have applied to many businesses and government offices in the city, hoping that through one of them God would give me work to do. But after two years I still have nothing. I am unemployed."

Her friends added that she was by no means the only one with this problem. They knew of at least two hundred university graduates who were currently looking for work, not counting those from other schools nearby. "Our parents back in the village worked hard to send us to school," they said. "We feel ashamed to go back with no jobs. We're just Bachelors of Unemployment."

"The more who graduate, the more are competing for jobs," Marmulia concluded. "It gets worse every year. But still I keep praying that God will give me work."

She turned to the pastor. "What is the Church's attitude toward unemployment?"

He didn't answer, but the question continued to trouble him. He wondered if it would do any good to bring it up to the Church Council.

Chapter 3

The Dilemmas of Development

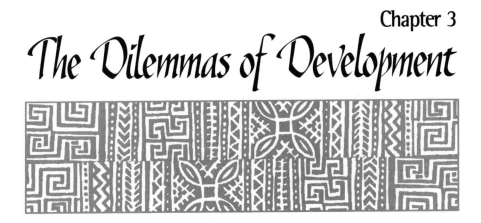

One of the words most often heard in Indonesian public discourse is *pem-bangunan*, "development." "National development based on Pancasila and the 1945 Constitution" punctuates every speech and serves as the common goal toward which all government programs are directed and the basis on which all decisions are justified. To be against development is equivalent to treason. In the abstract, who could disagree? All people want a better life for themselves and their children.

The problem comes when people want different things. Who then has the privilege of defining *development?* Up to the present, definition has been the sole prerogative of the government. Through a network of regional and national planning boards and a series of five-year plans, the national government has placed almost every aspect of public life within a grand scheme of national development. Implementation of the plan is required of government bureaucrats at every level; they in turn are expected to elicit the participation of the people, all under the protective wing of the military, the "stabilizer and dynamizer" of national development.

Judged by its own goals, the government's plan has been very successful. In outline, it goes something like this: By selling natural resources and encouraging foreign investment, Indonesia gains the capital needed to build an infrastructure of roads, electrical power, telecommunications, factories, schools, and hospitals. As the industrial base is built up, Indonesia will import fewer manufactured goods because it will be able to produce them in-country. Ownership of the means of production increasingly will be in the hands of the Indonesian business class, and their wealth will filter down to benefit the rest of the populace, who will then provide a thriving domestic market for Indonesian-made consumer goods. When this happens

John Campbell-Nelson

Development can mean a stable water supply so women need not resort to draining a banana stump in time of drought, as in this scene on Flores.

(according to Walter Lippman's theory, which has been the inspiration for the latter phases of the plan), the economy will have reached the "take-off" point, and further growth will be self-generated. Indonesia will have become a "developed" country.

In order to achieve these goals, however, sacrifices must be made. Agricultural prices must be kept down so that industrial workers and civil servants can still afford to eat. Industrial wages must be kept low to attract foreign investment, and all natural resources must be placed at the government's disposal. And finally, there must be tight restrictions on personal and political freedoms to ensure the cooperation of all citizens.

Remarkably, everything has gone pretty much according to plan. Indonesian industry is now a strong export engine, and leaders in business and government have achieved great personal wealth. Many see the current unrest, the demands for better wages and more political freedom, as a sign that the Plan has succeeded, and if people will only be patient a little longer, all will be well. Not everyone agrees, however. An apparently growing number of citizens seem to feel that they will never receive their fair share of the benefits of development unless they organize themselves into a powerful enough force to wrest it from the hands of the ruling class.

There is yet a third group that has both the ruling class and the opposition puzzled. It consists mainly of the indigenous peoples of the Outer Islands—the Dayaks of Kalimantan, West Papuans, Timorese, and many others. They do not seem to know what "development" is, and they're not sure they want it, at least not unless they can have it on their own terms. Their experience of development thus far has consisted of seeing their forests and mountains stripped bare by logging and mining interests, hearing their traditions ridiculed as backward, and seeing their children go off to school in regional towns only to return as strangers—or not to return at all. These people are the Indonesians I know best. How they have faced (or faced off) the bulldozers of development is the subject of this chapter.

My family lived in Timor for nearly twelve years, and during that time we were adopted into a Timorese family who live in the interior of South Central Timor, in a remote hamlet called Lelobatan. Grandpa Nicodemus, Grandma Maria, Petrus, Termutis, Ema, Magdalina, Ande, Ira, Yorem, Nola . . . it is a large extended family and they are all farmers and cattle herders. They were our teachers about the history and culture of Timor, our healers when we contracted a local illness, and our community of celebration for birthdays, Christmas, and Easter.

The essentials of their lives are virtually free of modern technology. They have no electricity, no cars or trucks, no television; the only running water is the mountain stream that flows near the house. Their farm implements consist of the digging stick, the hoe, and the machete. They do have a brick house with doors and real glass windows, but it is used chiefly for receiving guests—the family prefer to sleep and socialize around the cooking fires in their traditional beehive-shaped thatched houses.

The two kinds of house are symbolic of the family's attitude toward "modernity." They absorb aspects of the new, but rarely do they allow it to touch the core of their lives. Part of the reason is that they value their independence so highly. One day when Grandpa Nicodemus was lighting his home-grown cigarette with a flint and tinder, I asked him why he didn't just use a match. He laughed and said, "Why would I want to depend on a store for something as basic as fire?" In fact, he does use matches, but in typical parabolic fashion he wanted to make a point to the younger generation.

One day a Javanese friend of ours came to Lelobatan for a visit. She looked with awe at the size of the gardens, the variety of fruit trees, the growing coffee and spices, the cattle, pigs and chickens. As she was leaving, she said to me, "You know, with a little more knowledge of modern farming techniques they could really develop this place." When I related her comment to Petrus (Nicodemus' son and apprentice patriarch), he laughed. "What is it that we lack? At most we buy batteries for our flashlights and a little soap in the market. Just about everything else we produce for ourselves."

This pride in self-sufficiency has been necessary for survival in Lelobatan. Only in the past two decades has this remote mountain village been accessible to motorized vehicles. The development of a money economy, a market for agricultural products, and shops where people can buy manufactured goods is equally new to Nicodemus' family and, in their view, not entirely to be trusted. They live by the motto, "Don't eat your seed corn." The basic principle of their economy is that every family should retain control of the means of production for the basic necessities of life.

Agriculture in this area of Timor is a mixture of cultivated and forest farming. There are fields of rice, cassava, maize, peanuts, garlic, coriander, some vegetables, and rows and rows of citrus trees. Produce from the forests includes bamboo, coffee, hot peppers, wild game, and many herbs, both for cooking and for medicine. Building materials for traditional houses are also gathered from the forest, and because the forest is considered common property open to the use of all, there are virtually no homeless people in Timor. One evening I sat down with the family to list the names of trees and plants that they either grow on their land or gather from the forest. We finally stopped at over 120. Food is grown primarily for consumption by the family. Cash for taxes, health care, and school expenses comes from the livestock that graze on the surrounding hillsides and from the sale of oranges and garlic. This area of Timor is also known as cattle country. About 80 percent of the land is wooded with open pastures scattered intermittently through the forests.

About three kilometers (two miles) up the hill from Lelobatan is a prominent peak, Nau Sus (meaning, "from whence the milk flows"), that has served generations of Timorese as a religious site. Forests around the foot of this mountain were traditionally protected for the use of livestock and to preserve the watershed; it was taboo to turn the soil and plant in this area.

And then, in 1992, came "development." For the first time ever, this protected

Development is likely to mean destruction of the rain forest, as in Irian Jaya, to benefit the government or corporations, leading to ecological disaster, including drought and hunger for animals and tribal peoples.

area has been fenced off and farmers have been told to plant gardens here, on a short-term basis, as part of a government scheme to "regreen" this already quite green, forested land. To understand this irony a brief look at Indonesia's forestry policies is helpful.

By law, all natural resources are the property of the government, no matter whose land they are on. In the case of tribal lands, the problem is exacerbated by the fact that there is no legal certainty about who owns them, since ownership is determined by oral tradition not recognized by the government. More than 80 percent of the land in the interior of Timor and other islands has never been surveyed or registered. As a convenient shortcut, many regional authorities have simply declared that all lands not under cultivation are the property of the government. If there are any trees on these lands, they are under supervision of the forestry department, which is then free to sell them off to timber concessions. The need to stimulate the economy easily overshadows calls for a well-developed and carefully implemented policy regarding the status and use of Indonesia's forests, which are also homeland for hundreds of indigenous tribes—including our family in Lelobatan.

In a country whose mammoth government is rampant with corruption and has begun to feel the squeeze for lack of domestic revenues, you can imagine the environmental nightmare created by twenty years of abused forestry concessions. Just three years ago vast areas of wooded hillside were deforested in a scheme to replant with fast-growing pulpwood for paper manufacture and with tropical hardwoods such as mahogany and teak for manufacture of furniture and plywood. It should surprise no one to learn that the paper mills are largely owned by Suharto's children. It is never clear where the native wood that is cut down goes, and in most cases no one bothers to find out. Ironically, this massive clearcutting of native forest was done under the name of "reforestation."

When the tentacles of a government-backed program for developing such an "industrial forest plantation" reached Lelobatan (again in the guise of reforestation), my family didn't pay much attention at first. Oh sure, a barbed-wire fence now lined the muddy road into Lelobatan and fields *had* begun to crop up around the foot of Nau Sus, but we had also heard the area had been targeted as a tourist attraction. It was hard to imagine that the beautiful vistas that had become a second home to us could really be endangered. Having witnessed a number of failed development projects in other places it was easy to hope that this scheme too would fail.

But then we began to hear stories of how cattle found inside the barbed wire were butchered and how the fence was to be extended for miles and miles. Without consulting the local populace as required by law, local forestry officials had claimed nearly 800 hectares (about 1,900 acres) of mostly forested land, part of the main watershed for South Central Timor and the pasture for all the farmers' livestock. Timorese we know and love were scared. What was to happen to their cattle and to them? If the government's project was really a regreening project, why wasn't severely eroded land in the area being targeted instead of acres of pasture land? Was it possible that the real target of this project was the centuries-old tropical hardwood forest that already covered much of the land? If it was, Grandpa Nicodemus knew it meant that the water would dry up and so would the world he had always known.

Timorese culture is rooted in tradition. Once ruled by a king, the Timorese now obey their modern rulers, the governor along with his regional administrators. Although Timorese may complain a lot in private about government policy, they tend to do whatever it takes to keep the government off their backs. That means not attracting attention, keeping quiet, "going with the flow" of city-orchestrated policies and decisions when those decisions touch their lives. There is no tradition of direct confrontation or protest except within or between tribes. Crossing the government simply isn't heard of. So what does one do when one's cattle and extended family's cattle and neighbor's cattle—the "life savings" of thousands of Timorese—are suddenly threatened? My wife, Karen Campbell-Nelson, wrote the following account of the eventual confrontation:

THE POWER OF NO PRAYER

My birthday is in September. This year, because John and I knew it was only a matter of weeks before we would leave Timor (due to visa problems), we invited friends to Lelobatan to celebrate. Part of the celebration included an informal meeting of young clergy, former students of mine and John's, who now serve village congregations throughout South Central Timor. This was our second gathering for sharing and discussion. Although John and I had no concrete agenda for this group, it was our hope that they could grow into a forum that would foster church-based social action at the grass roots. We had intentionally kept the group small and our gatherings informal.

A few days before my birthday our close friend Petrus informed us that on the day of my birthday celebration there was also to be a service of dedication and blessing for the official opening of the government's regreening program. A small handful of farmers went to discuss their concern with the local magistrate a day before the opening, but instead of being received, they were passed from bureaucrat to bureaucrat, one of whom had the gall to suggest they might consider transmigrating to another island.

Just hours before the government's ceremony was to begin up the hill from where we were staying, we met with the Timorese pastors and a few friends from a legal advocacy group whom we had also invited. Discussion of problems faced by Timorese villagers included forced sterilization to meet family-planning targets (the government is trying to slow population growth), the "legal" confiscation of sandalwood by the government, abuses in recent elections, and, of course, the current land crisis around Nau Sus. The pastors were not surprised because they had witnessed similar situations in other areas of Timor, but they were angry and were concerned about their friend Bendalina, the young pastor who served Lelobatan and its surrounding villages. Why hadn't she shown up yet? Was she planning to attend the dedication ceremony?

Since the church and government in South Central Timor have cordial relations, at least on the surface, most government events include not only the presence of a pastor but the expectation of a prayer of blessing as well. Such a blessing is much more than a mere formality; in Timor no one would feel safe conducting any major project without first seeking a divine blessing. Our young friends suspected that Bendalina had been asked to give the blessing, and they longed for a chance to discuss strategy with her before the ceremony was to begin. But she had not appeared, and because we had heard that she had been sick we wondered if she would attempt the seven-kilometer (five-mile) hike from her home on the other side of Nau Sus. When a number of officials from the local forestry department showed up at noon, apparently looking for Reverend Bendalina, things began to feel tense. John's and my presence as Westerners was regarded with suspicion, and John even had his photo taken by a police intelligence officer. Police efforts to get Grandpa Nicodemus to implicate us in some sort of antigovernment protest failed, and they eventually left.

Invigorated by our morning discussions, and angered by these officials' efforts to intimidate the family hosting us, some of the young pastors decided to attend the ceremony in hopes of raising their concerns with the government officials. We had begun our sharing that morning with a brief meditation on Psalm 24:

> The earth is the Lord's and all that is in it, the world, and those who live
> in it;
> for he has founded it on the seas, and established it on the rivers.
> Who shall ascend the hill of the Lord? And who shall stand in his holy place?
> Those who have clean hands and pure hearts, who do not lift up their souls
> to what is false, and do not swear deceitfully.
> They will receive blessing from the Lord, and vindication from the God of
> their salvation.

Local farmers, accompanied by these pastors, headed up the hillside. One pastor, editor of the church newsletter, *Berita GMIT*, took along a camera. Another friend, a woman from the church's development and agricultural training center, carried a tape recorder. And still Bendalina, the woman whom the government expected to bless this whole fiasco with a solemn, public prayer, had not appeared.

Within thirty minutes Bendalina came. She was tired and a bit hoarse, having hiked many mountain miles during the past week to perform marriage ceremonies in the eight village congregations she serves. She had indeed been notified by the government to pray for the opening of the regreening project. Many of the farmers in her congregations had been bitterly complaining about the project, and she understood the threat it posed, both environmentally and culturally. She also knew what was expected of her by the government. And she knew that if she could refuse to pray, she would give courage and strength to those who feared to make their protest public.

Even as Bendalina was asking me and John what she ought to do, the head of the project himself appeared at the house to escort her up the hill. The opening could not proceed without a blessing. Bendalina asked me and two other women friends who had not joined the others on the hillside to pray with her. We huddled in a small circle and prayed for Bendalina. We prayed for her to have the courage to speak the truth, to serve her people with integrity. All four of us cried and hugged one another. Then we dried our eyes and Bendalina was gone.

While preparations were proceeding for my evening birthday celebration, some sort of confrontation was happening up the mountainside. Those of us below waited anxiously for several hours, wondering what could possibly be taking so long. Would Bendalina in the end pray or not?

Just before sundown four of the pastors came running back with shouts of victory. By refusing to pray a false prayer Bendalina had effectively denied the church's blessing on a poorly conceived and exploitative government project. Once Bendalina had spoken, other pastors and village elders rose to voice their concern and then walked out on the proceedings, leaving uneaten the feast the government had prepared. The forestry officials went back to the city, threatening to return with the army if the people persisted in their opposition. John and I were thrilled, encouraged, and filled with hope that close friends, leaders of local churches, were able to give one another mutual support and encouragement to take a stand for justice. It was one of the best birthday presents I've ever had.

The next morning, after an evening of food, song, dance, and merriment, our pastor friends gathered for a parting prayer. Spontaneously and with great gusto they burst out singing "We've a story to tell to the nations, that shall turn their hearts to the right" (which until then had never been among my Top 10 of favorite hymns). John and I looked at each other and grinned. It was one of those rare moments when I knew the Holy Spirit was at hand.

The conflict continued for four years. Hundreds of cattle died for lack of forage; people went without medical care and children postponed further schooling for lack of funds. But in the end, the people won. Their strategy of resistance might be called "accepting in order to reject." When the vice governor came with a military escort, they assured him that they would support the government's plans on the condition that none of the existing trees would be cut down. Then they scared off the workers the forestry department had hired to do the fencing and planting and offered to do the work themselves. This they did, but they placed the fence posts only a few inches deep; during the day they planted seedlings and at night they let their cattle in. When a seedling began to grow, a gentle tug on the stem was enough to break the root hairs. They prayed to God to withhold the rain, and God apparently obliged, for the following two years saw an uncharacteristic drought. At last, the forestry department gave up in despair and went off in search of "greener pastures." The barbed wire has been salvaged for other uses, and the cattle again graze freely on the green hillsides. And the forest still stands.

Analysis and Interpretation: Understanding the Villagers

At great cost to themselves, the people of Lelobatan and surrounding villages thus managed to fight off "development." Other villages have not been so successful, and the destruction of native forest to make way for the monoculture of trees for industrial use continues. The heart of the issue is not whether to develop but who decides what kind of development will be promoted. The peasants hold to the idea that development means maintaining control of the means of production, improving their methods of subsistence agriculture, and seeking a fair price for their cattle and crops. The government's plan calls for exploitation of natural resources for the sake of industrialization. In this view, the indigenous peoples are what economists call an "externality." At best they are in the way, and at worst they are a threat.

It might even be argued that the modern Indonesian economy is not one economy but two. The industrial, capital-intensive, market-oriented, commodity-for-export, money-driven modern economy dominates national development policy. But only a minority of Indonesians are directly involved in this economy, and its benefits are distributed very unevenly. Around the edges of this dominant new economy is the centuries-old economy of subsistence agriculture, which includes nearly 90 per-

cent of the people of the Outer Islands and millions of Javanese rice farmers as well. They provide food to the dominant economy and it rewards them with a few modern amenities, but the two economies remain distinct. Finally, there is the growing mass of people who have left the traditional economy, either because they have sought higher education or because they have lost their land, but who have not found a place within the modern economy. They are in the most difficult position of all.

Action: Choices for North Americans

For North Americans, this problem may seem remote. The United States is, after all, one of the premier industrial nations, and its agriculture has itself become another sector of industry. To find an example of the conflict in Lelobatan we would have

Village elders are losing their authority as the Indonesian government takes over tribal lands and sends Javanese and other settlers to the Outer Islands.

Karen Campbell-Nelson

to go back several centuries. In pre-industrial England every village had an area known as the commons. It was a preserve of natural resources available to all people without regard to ownership, open to grazing and to hunting and gathering of forest products. Its use was usually regulated by a council of local residents. Beginning in the fifteenth century, the aristocracy increasingly claimed personal ownership of the commons and fenced it off in order to raise sheep to provide wool for the growing textile industry. They also enclosed fields that the peasants had grown crops on for themselves and the nobles. Denied the use of the commons and the fields, the peasants were forced to go to the cities to sell their labor in the mills. It was the suffering of these workers that first inspired Karl Marx in the nineteenth century to reflect on the exploitive nature of capitalism.

Perhaps few today among the American or Canadian middle class would ever ask, "What do we lack?" as Petrus did, because there is always a new car, a new TV, or some other commodity just on the horizon of our expectations. But the contrast can be instructive. Petrus and his village were fighting to retain the commons, because it was essential to preserving their way of life and, in economic terms, to retaining control of the means of sustaining that life. Very few North Americans "control the means of production" that sustain any aspect of their lives. A poor Timorese can still build a house of materials gathered from the commons, but the homeless in the United States and Canada are reduced to scavenging cardboard boxes. Despite our reverence for the "entrepreneurial spirit," most of us simply sell our labor or our expertise to whoever will employ us, pretty much on the employer's terms. We vote, but many of us have concluded that corporate interests have more to say about government policy than the voice of the electorate. And we have virtually nothing at all to say about corporate policy. Our political franchise pales before our economic disempowerment. Perhaps there is indeed something that we lack after all. Perhaps just as Petrus fought to retain his economic rights, so we must fight to regain them.

The twenty-fourth psalm asserts a basic principle of our religious heritage. It says that "The earth is the Lord's, and all that is in it." Christians further maintain that God gave the earth for the common good of all living things. But today, global capitalism has privatized God's creation, right down to the genetic level—there are even patents on life forms. The commons is closed and in its traditional agrarian form would do us little good now, anyway. Most of us would not be capable of a lifestyle like that of the people of Lelobatan. We lack the skills, and probably the inclination. Nonetheless, we might do well to reflect on the trade-offs involved: a low-tech, low-consumption, communal self-sufficiency versus a high-tech, high-consumption, individualistic lifestyle that is also highly dependent on corporatism. For North Americans even to have a choice, we would have to reinvent the commons in some new, postindustrial form.

Historically, we seem to have opted for "the fleshpots of Egypt" over life in the wilderness, even if Egypt means enslavement to Pharaoh. But shouldn't indigenous peoples have a right not to "develop" on Pharaoh's terms? God thought so, if the book of Exodus is any evidence.

Chapter 4

From Barter to Cash

The winds of change do not blow only in the cities. Although the basic practices of subsistence agriculture in rural Indonesia have remained much the same for centuries, within the last thirty years a number of factors have converged to produce what local sailors call *angin panca roba*—"winds from five directions." The availablility of immunizations and the increase in rural health clinics have reduced the mortality rate and produced a rural population explosion. Indonesia's great achievement of providing nearly universal primary education (it is theoretically "free" but many fees are still levied) has opened new horizons to rural youth, although it has not necessarily given them the means to take advantage of these new opportunities. An expanded market for agricultural commodities, high-yield strains of seed, and government promotion of fertilizer and pesticides have begun to change traditional farming practices. The availablility of consumer goods in rural marketplaces has also expanded rapidly. But perhaps the most fundamental force for change is also one of the most subtle: the development of the money economy.

North Americans are so accustomed to dealing with money that it is difficult for us to imagine a world without it. But until recently money played a marginal role in rural Indonesia, especially in the Outer Islands. The Dutch had introduced silver coins to aid commerce and as a medium of taxation, but they remained on the edges of rural life. The coins were more often treated as precious metal and used for decorations or melted down for jewelry. If you had taxes to pay, it was necessary to trade a cow or a weaving in order to obtain coins. But even in these cases "money" was just one more item of trade within a system dominated by barter. Wealth was measured by the amount of food in the storehouse and cattle in the pasture.

Perhaps of equal importance is the fact that wealth was measured in relationships. Within the clan, security was assured by distributing agricultural resources according to need among the extended family and in-laws. Outside the clan, people obtained what they could not produce for themselves by maintaining trade relationships with others who had what they needed. For the sake of developing these relationships it was not unusual in bartering to give more than one received. This surplus would establish a debt of gratitude that the trading partner would be expected to repay at a later time. It was a savings account of human relationships.

One of the major occasions for "squaring the accounts" in this rural barter economy was the festival. Weddings, funerals, house-raisings, peacemaking after a conflict—all provided opportunity for villagers to redistribute the wealth, repay debts, and reaffirm relationships. If you brought a cow to my wedding feast, I would bring a cow and a pig to yours. In a world without refrigeration, these feasts were also the major source of protein in the diet.

A friend once held such a feast when he needed to re-thatch the roof on his house. All the extended family, neighbors, and in-laws gathered for three days to do the work, during which he fed them with vast amounts of rice and meat. He told me that it was costing him twice as much as it would have if he had simply hired laborers to do the job. "So why do it this way?" was my obvious question. "If we don't gather to help each other, how will we know we're a family?" he said. "Money has no family."

In a barter economy, cows can be traded for a bride or other desired goods. Shelter can be built from materials at hand so no one need be homeless.

An economist couldn't have put it better. The very things that make money so useful in a market economy are detrimental to an economy based on relationships. Money is quantified in a way that items for barter and exchange rarely are. Owing a debt of gratitude can be scaled to the ability to pay in a way that monetary debts are not: a poor person can bring a chicken to a feast while a rich one brings a cow, but both eat from the same pot. Money is anonymous; no relationship nor even a conversation is required to make a purchase. Perhaps most significant, money is portable. A cow cannot be zapped electronically to an account in Jakarta. Especially in rural economies, cash exchanges tend to flow out of the local economy, whereas bartered exchanges circulate within it.

The effects of the spread of a money economy in rural areas are many and complex. It has introduced strains on the solidarity of the clan by encouraging individuals to accumulate cash wealth rather than investing their resources in the community. And indeed the community can no longer supply all the needs of its members as it once did. Money literally does not grow on trees, and that means that farmers must grow something they can sell for cash to pay for school fees, medicines, and consumer goods. The traditional cycle of feasts, once a balanced system of social give and take, has become an economic liability. This economic shift is the background to the following case study. It was adapted from *Studi Kasus Pastoral,* Vol. 2: *Nusa Tenggara Timur* (BPK Gunung Mulia, 1990), a book written by a group of pastors from eastern Indonesia and translated by Dra. Anne Hommes. They were concerned about the effect of moneylenders not only on the rural economy but on the rural churches as well. The events take place on the island of Sumba but are typical of many other rural areas of eastern Indonesia.

LOAN SHARKS IN THE CONGREGATION

The soil is not fertile in the eastern part of the Indonesian archipelago. The land is barren, rocky, and mountainous. Farm plots are small, producing mostly maize and in some places rice. Simple traditional tools are used. The rainy season is short with little precipitation. Because of drought the harvest often fails, causing famine. Under these harsh conditions, people will move away from their village to seek work elsewhere, leaving their family behind. This has a negative impact on family life. It also draws men to gambling in order to make a fast buck, or to borrow money on their crops before they are harvested, a practice called the *ijon* system.

Centuries-old customs such as wedding and burial ceremonies are still being honored. Bride-price and traditional celebrations demand large amounts of money from the family. In order to meet these costs, the family does not hesitate to go into debt by borrowing. However, the interest asked by the lender can be high. The precious cash gained from selling the harvest is then used to pay off this debt instead of providing for the family needs, a situation that aggravates the existing state of poverty.

The government makes an effort to break this cycle of poverty by establishing village cooperatives. These would safeguard a fair market price for the harvest, instead of its being sold too cheaply by individual farmers in need of cash.

The churches have shown little initiative in alleviating poverty and hunger. Although they are aware of their mission to lighten suffering and poverty, their pattern of pastoral ministry remains focused on doctrine and moral admonishment rather than social action. The following case illustrates the bind the church finds itself in regarding social ministry.

Most church members of the village of Tanambara are farmers. Their only means of livelihood is their *sawah* (ricefield), which yields a crop once a year due to the short rainy season. The soil in Tanambara does not lend itself to growing other crops such as corn or yams. The cash the farmers earn from the harvest will enable them to provide for the family's needs, pay their church pledge, and fulfil their cultural obligations for weddings and funerals.

Because farmers often do not make enough profit selling their rice to provide all these necessities, they may turn to a moneylender. From January till May some merchants or other well-to-do people will offer the farmer cash in exchange for rice at the time of the harvest, plus a high interest. To borrow the cash value of one kilo (two pounds) of rice the farmer will have to repay with two or three kilos (four or six pounds) of rice at the harvest time. Many of these moneylenders are not outsiders but villagers. Some of them are church members and even church officers, but they charge the same high interest rates. At harvest time in July or August the lenders, including church officials, seize the rice crop of the parishioners, who then find themselves in poverty again, trapped in a vicious circle by this *ijon* system.

The church's ministry is also affected by poverty. The collections during worship are small, forcing the congregation to pay its lay pastor and assistant less and less either in cash or in kind. Church attendance drops because many members are desperately trying to make a living. The preacher, be it the lay pastor or a church elder, only talks about getting out of this circle of poverty. No action to help is ever undertaken.

When the pastor of the church at Tanambara visited Barnabas, one of the church members, the following conversation took place:

Pastor: "Barnabas, I have not seen you in church lately. You are also very far behind on your pledge."

Barnabas: "You are right, pastor. The problem is, what would my family and I wear to church? We have no decent clothes left. I'm often in the forest looking for wild yams to eat. Our rice supply is all in hock to the merchants."

Pastor: "Oh, I see. But why are you in debt? Don't you know that borrowing money on your crop is a sin, which the church opposes? A Christian should be in church, putting money in the collection."

Barnabas: "What to do, pastor? My children have to eat. I have to pay for their schooling. The village cooperative is short of money and cannot pay a decent price for our rice. The church doesn't help. If you have only come to preach to me and not to help, I would rather go to the loan sharks. At least my family won't go hungry."

Analysis: Understanding Village Traditions

The church in Tanambara was established in 1967 with 20 members. In 1974 the government designated Tanambara as an official location for resettling scattered rural residents in "concentrated villages." Housing was built and each new settler was given two hectares (five acres) to farm. The population grew, and by 1986 church membership had risen to 210. The members were rice farmers. They had a grade-school education or were illiterate. Many factors contribute to their poverty.

One of the chief factors is the *ijon* system of pledging one's harvest as security to obtain a short-term loan, often at a high interest rate. The loan can take the form of rice or other foodstuffs, credit at a merchant's store, or cash. The interest rate can be double or triple the amount loaned. At harvest time, the crop is either delivered directly to the moneylender or sold to another buyer and the cash used to pay off the loan. Thus most profits from the rice harvest go directly to the moneylenders, leaving little for the farmers' daily expenses.

Another factor contributing to poverty is the malfunctioning of the village cooperative. The cooperative cannot absorb the village harvest because it has insufficient funds to buy the crop and has only one rice mill to serve about 10,000 members. Farmers must dispose of their harvest even if they sell at a loss. Therefore, rice merchants have the upper hand.

The church sits on the economic sideline. Financially weak, it conducts a traditional ministry, which emphasizes the spiritual life. It teaches church members to endure daily hardship while awaiting happiness in heaven. The church is just awakening to its mission to liberate people from poverty and other forms of oppression, but it has not done much more than preach about it.

The atttitude of the local farmers also plays an important role in continuing the practice of *ijon* and thus their poverty. For them, borrowing is a normal procedure. Poverty is one's fate.

The traditional kinship system contributes indirectly to the villagers' poverty. Kinship in Tanambara includes relationships within the nuclear family, the extended family, the clan, and the neighborhood.

In Tanambara the nuclear family is part of an extended family of several generations and siblings' families living under one roof. They support and help one another, not just in the daily tasks but also in meeting obligations for weddings, funerals, and other ceremonies. Such ceremonies are attended by the whole clan, a network of extended families connected by marriage. By helping to celebrate such important occasions, clan members, even those living at a distance, maintain their clan identity.

Such celebrations are expensive. The wedding ceremony, for example, is performed in three stages. First the man's family approaches the woman's family to ask

Weddings are costly affairs that cause many families to go into debt for years in order to maintain their social standing and religious tradition.

for her hand. As a bride-price they bring several cows, horses, water buffalos, and gold or silver jewelry. The woman's family slaughters and roasts a pig and a number of weavings are exchanged. Next the bride's family considers the bride-price brought by the man's family. Hard bargaining takes place. Finally, an acceptable amount of cattle is agreed upon, possibly up to a hundred. The marriage is finalized in a traditional ceremony. Then comes a church wedding followed by an elaborate and costly feast.

Funerals are also elaborate and expensive. Most people in Tanambara, whether or not they are Christians, when they die remain in the home for as long as several weeks awaiting the arrival of faraway relatives. During that time the mourners, already assembled and arriving, are fed daily by the dead person's family, who slaughter many cattle. The clan must shoulder these ceremonial expenses, which can run high.

Clearly, the demands of traditional ceremonies add to the poverty in Tanambara. How to make sense of this? This leads us into the next part, interpretation.

Interpretation: A Christian Understanding of the Tanambara Poor

The harmony of the congregation is disturbed by the existence of two groups with different interests—the hungry farmers, who are continually in debt, and the rich rice merchants and moneylenders, who are benefiting from the farmers' misfortune. The situation is made even more critical, because members of the church board, as participants in the *ijon* system, are exploiting their brothers in Christ.

The Poor in the Bible

The plight of the Tanambara farmers is neatly described in the Bible: "The fields of the poor yield much food; but it is swept away through injustice" (Prov. 13:23). The early Israelites were wandering herders with little distinction between rich and poor. Only after they settled in Canaan did poverty emerge. As Israel developed economically during the age of the monarchy, a large share of the wealth was pocketed by a few, while the common people remained poor. Laws were made to protect the poor (Lev. 25:35–37), but they did not succeed in preventing economic injustice. Prophets such as Amos (chaps. 2–6) and Isaiah (1:23) criticized the rich and powerful for their injustice to the poor.

Nevertheless, the Old Testament makes clear that riches and poverty are not only caused by external forces or determined by fate. In the wisdom literature, such as Proverbs, Solomon's wealth is the result of his wisdom. The poor are accused of laziness (Prov. 6:6 ff) and unwillingness to learn: "Whoever loves pleasure will suffer want" (Prov. 21:17).

In the apocalyptic books, the emphasis on salvation at the end of the world puts a new value on suffering and poverty. People who suffer are encouraged to endure it since it is the result of living in a sinful world. Their attention should be directed toward the time when a new world will emerge without poverty or hunger. These apocalyptic books hold promises for the poor yet pious. Their fate will change for the better at the endtime, when the Messiah comes (see I Enoch 96:1 ff).

The promise of radical change can also be seen in Mary's song of praise: "He brought down mighty kings from their thrones and lifted up the lowly" (Luke 1:52 ff). Or in the letter of James: "And now, you rich people, listen to me. Weep and wail over the miseries that are coming upon you!" (5:1).

Like the prophets, Jesus sided with the poor, while the rich were cursed. As in the apocalyptic books, Jesus promised the poor the kingdom of God, except that in Jesus the kingdom of God already is realized in this world. Jesus' promise is not one to be fulfilled later, but rather one that should be visible now in the life of the church. This attitude of Jesus is expressed in the Beatitudes found in Matthew and Luke: "Blessed are you who are poor; for yours is the kingdom of God. Blessed are you who are hungry now, for you will be filled. Blessed are you who weep now, for you will laugh" (Luke 6:20, 21). The parallelism between the one who is poor, the one who is hungry, and the one who is weeping reveals that the meaning of "poor" is the one who suffers, who is needy in an economic and social sense (compare also Isa. 61:1).

Of course, poor people are not declared happy only because they are poor. They are declared happy because they are open to the coming of God's kingdom (Matt. 5:3).

They have no earthly powers or obstacles that cause them to ignore the call to repentence. To the poor, God is their only hope, since there is no help from elsewhere.

The Poor in Tanambara

There are similarities between the needy in the Bible and the Tanambara farmers victimized by the merchants. These farmers need God's help because human help and concern have slipped away. Yet they are not merely victims. They also bring misfortune on themselves by continuing the old, traditional customs. They have adjusted themselves to overspending on traditional ceremonies that they cannot afford. They are willing to work, but they do not heed the advice: "He who loves pleasure will be a poor man" (Prov. 21:17). Be that as it may, they are clearly victims of merchants, who do not intend to help them but only to seek personal gain.

The religious beliefs of the farmers and merchants in Tanambara have intensified their respective situations. Pastors have a tendency to spiritualize terms such as "poor" and "meek" in the manner of the apocalyptic books. They preach that pious people who currently suffer in this world will be compensated in the hereafter. As a popular hymn puts it: "Although in deep trouble now, one day we will be without cares and joyful." They make no effort to improve the farmers' situation.

The farmers, who see the merchants enjoying the fruits of the farmers' labor, do not turn to the church for help but rather say, "It is not necessary for the church to interfere in the *ijon* system." The church's business is salvation in the life hereafter. At the same time, they accept the burden of large expenditures in order to conform

Most residents of this Batak village on Sumatra do not have cash to buy station wagons and satellite dishes.

with traditional local customs. This clinging to tradition is contrary to the freedom brought by Christ and is a serious obstacle to combatting poverty in Tanambara.

The merchants, like the rich people criticized by Amos, believe that the right relationship with God does not depend on good deeds toward others but is a matter of the heart. So they can praise God in their hymn singing, while at the same time they live well off the fruits of somebody else's labor. They are like those people going to church thinking: "When will . . . the Sabbath [be over] so that we may offer wheat for sale? We will . . . practice deceit with false balances, buying the poor for silver . . . and selling the sweepings of the wheat" (Amos 8:5).

Actually, in the life of the church, faith and deeds cannot be separated. Paul indeed emphasizes that only faith can save. But clearly faith is made visible through acts of love (Gal. 5:6). Matthew says the same: Jesus will say to the righteous people, "Come, you that are blessed by my Father, inherit the kingdom . . . for I was hungry and you gave me food" (Matt. 25:34, 35). God allowed himself to be met in the needy who suffer. Love for God is made manifest in love for one's neighbor.

Similarly, God can be met in the poor of Tanambara. "If one member [of the body] suffers, all suffer together with it" (1 Cor. 12:26). As a member of the body of Christ, the Christian is responsible for the well-being of all the other members. It is showing contempt for God's fellowship of believers when part of the congregation is hungry and others eat and drink abundantly, putting those who have nothing to shame. In short, such a situation stains the body of Christ (1 Cor. 11:21, 22).

Action: What the Church Can Do

The church could work in many areas to improve the lot of its poorer members.

Aid to Cooperatives and Other Development Agencies

Rich church members (merchants and moneylenders) could not possibly be expected to help poor members because it would be contrary to the rich members' self-interest. But the pastor and the church board could help the farmers form a rice cooperative, where they could borrow rice against their coming harvest at a low interest rate. Thus they would avoid the high interest rates of the *ijon* moneylenders, and the poor would be helping the poor. There is a liberating and empowering aspect when the poor become aware that they can help one another.

The church could also cooperate with government agencies concerned with development. For example, it could work with the existing village cooperative set up by the government, to try to find an alternative to the *ijon* system. The church could make the following suggestions:

- The cooperative could encourage the farmers to sell their rice only to the cooperative.
- The cooperative could oblige the merchants to buy their supply of rice only through the cooperative.
- The church council could turn to a higher government body to make more funds available to the cooperative.

The church could also cooperate with other governmental agencies such as the department of agriculture to teach the farmers how to increase their rice yield, to improve the quality of the rice so it would fetch a higher price on the market, or to raise other crops.

The church could also join forces with nongovernmental rural development agencies, such as the Indonesian Welfare Institute, Church World Service, and others, in order to promote farming skills, self-help programs, and other development projects.

Downscaling of Traditional Ceremonies

In regard to local traditions, the church is caught between contradictory views. On one hand, it preaches liberation from the constraints of tradition. On the other hand, it cannot serve the local people without regard for the culture of Sumba. Neither the abolition of costly traditional ceremonies nor their uncritical preservation is the right action. There are other possibilities:

- gradually decreasing the extravagant expenses involved in weddings and funerals
- confering with the government about policies to decrease these ceremonial demands
- initiating a simplified version of these traditional practices

Training Program for Church Members

Finally, the church could plan and organize a training program for church members. The form and content should be adapted to the needs of the congregation.

- Such a program could introduce discussion on traditional customs, social justice, and other local issues, all seen from a Christian point of view.
- Action/reflection groups could focus on problems in the congregation.
- Church leaders could make pastoral visits and conversations, intentionally concentrating on traditional customs, *ijon*, and other related topics.
- The church board could suggest that the regional assembly and synod meeting discuss *ijon* in order to formulate the church's stance on it.

Any action should be carefully planned and integrated with the rest of the program in order to have the greatest impact.

Postscript

Since the writing of this case study nearly ten years ago, little has changed in Tanambara. The reason? Many of the members of the church board in question were themselves moneylenders. It is not easy to implement a plan that conflicts with one's own economic interests—even in the name of Christ.

Chapter 5

A Woman's Rights and a Man's Pride

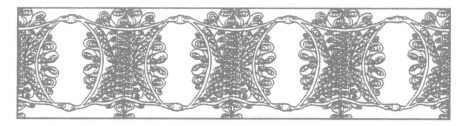

The women's movement in Indonesia began, as it did in the West, among the educated women of the middle and upper middle class. The foremother of the movement was Kartini, daughter of a Javanese aristocrat, who advocated the right of women to an education and carried on a lively correspondence with a variety of Dutch supporters at the beginning of the twentieth century. She has been elevated to the status of national hero and role model for modern Indonesian women.

Despite the Islamic context of Indonesia, there has rarely been the kind of veiling of women and circumscription of women's role in public life that are associated with the Arab countries. Many Indonesians would say such restrictions on women are more a reflection of Arab culture than of the teachings of Islam. Feminism, however, has few supporters in Indonesia. Most people prefer to see the issues of women's rights in the context of the relationship between women and men—hence the title of this chapter. Currently the women's movement in Indonesia seems to focus on two distinct groups: educated professionals of the middle class and women farmers and artisans of the villages. The former group will be the focus in this chapter, since the Indonesian middle class is little represented elsewhere in this book.

The following story of Hety and Tono and its interpretation and recommendations was adapted from a case study written by a group of pastors, theological educators, and lay people from Java. They held intensive conversations with Hety about events that took place between the late 1960s and the early 1980s.

WHAT WAS IT ALL FOR?

Hety and Tono come from central Java. Both are Christian. Tono comes from a traditional *priyayi* family (the *priyayi* class includes professionals, civil servants, and the traditional ruling class). Hety comes from a *priyayi* family that feels formal education for women is important. The two met and began going steady during their first year at a university. They decided to marry upon completion of their bachelor's degree, when they were only twenty-two. Because Hety had an opportunity to teach on one of the Outer Islands for an international organization, at a large salary, they left Java. Hety was pregnant at the time, and she and Tono knew they would need an income to prepare for the baby's birth. In their new location, Tono found a church position but with a much smaller salary than Hety's.

Actually, Tono, a traditional Javanese, didn't like his role as one who followed his wife. In addition, from the beginning he felt humiliated because, contrary to custom, all the wedding expenses and subsequent costs till their departure had been covered by his wife's family. He always felt second in the family.

In their new home, Tono rebelled by often leaving the house in search of recognition of his superior role as a man. Because he did not have an advanced degree and so was unlikely to win a big professional reputation, he sought recog-

In modern Indonesia a few fortunate women can earn professional degrees, like this new bachelor of divinity.

nition through youth and student organizations. He succeeded in getting elected the chair of an important mass organization, but there was no salary, and he was not at home to help Hety care for the house.

Before her child was born, Hety was able to take care of domestic duties while continuing to teach well. But things were different once the child arrived. Hety had a lot of bleeding during the birth and it was hard for her to breastfeed. To care for the child, run the household, and teach outside the home became too great a burden. What was more, in less than two months, since they did not use birth control, Hety became pregnant again. It was another difficult birth, complicated by an automobile accident. Because Hety still had to work, as well as caring for two children under a year old, her situation became increasingly painful. Hety's mother felt as if her daughter were being treated like a slave, but Hety defended her husband, saying that he was experiencing a crisis of self-respect and needed her help even if she had to suffer.

Because Tono was intelligent and creative, he finally got an opportunity to study in the United States. Hety was willing for him to go, hoping that he would discover a sense of self-worth once he earned a higher degree than hers. Tono hoped the church he worked for would support his wife and children while he was abroad. He asked for financial help, promising to serve the church upon his return. The church refused on the grounds that Tono had obtained his scholarship under his own auspices, not through church channels.

Tono left his wife and children at his parents' home in Java. According to custom, his parents were now responsible for them. Because the social-political climate in the country was unstable (when the government accused the Communists of plotting to overturn the government), Tono's family had lost much of its wealth. Furthermore, his parents still had the responsibility of caring for their ten younger children. Hety resolved to take care of her own household

It became apparent that the second child was suffering from a chronic condition that required continual medical care. Hety was forced to use up all her savings and sell what she could in order to pay for medicine, doctor's bills, and living expenses. A few months after Tono's departure, the child had to be hospitalized for forty days.

Fortunately, after one year, Tono was able to have Hety and his children join him at his university in the United States. Not long after he received his master's degree, his father died. Tono's family demanded he return home in order to help support the family. Tono seriously considered the demand, but Hety prayed hard and made a concerted effort to convince her husband to finish his doctorate, since he was unlikely to have another chance to do so. For this purpose she was willing to work to send money home to her husband's family.

Tono took his degree with high honors and was offered a position at the university, but with Hety's agreement he decided to return to his homeland to fulfill his duty to his family and country. He obtained ministerial work in Indonesia and enthusiastically they both agreed to live in an undeveloped region.

About a year later, their older child took sick, suffered intensely for a week, and died. Although outwardly calm, Hety felt full of anger and rebellion at this unavoidable misfortune. She was angry with her husband and with God. For nine years she had considered only other people. She had made an effort to be a good wife and mother by sacrificing her own career and freedom. But if the child she loved so much could so easily experience agony and be snatched from her, "In the end, what was all my sacrifice for?"

Analysis: Placing Hety and Tono in Indonesian Society

To understand Hety's despairing question, it is helpful to look at the traditions of upper-class Javanese society and the roles of men and women in it.

A wedding is a formal alliance of two families involving responsibilities and sacrifices for the sake of the whole family.

Javanese Ideals

In Javanese mystical thought, as discussed by N. Mulder in *Kebatinan dan Hidup Sehari-hari Orang Jawa* (Gramedia), 1984, the ideals of integration and harmony between humanity and God provide the model for relations between the individual and society. Accordingly, order, peace, and balance should be preserved at all costs; events are predictable; and good manners and harmony must be cultivated among all parts of a family and of society. Thus, behavior must be regulated, harmonious relations must be protected, and all open conflict must be avoided. For the sake of harmony, an individual must put aside personal desires for the sake of the greater whole. Consequently the Javanese highly respect self-control. A person who is perfectly able to control himself or herself is said to be *sembodho*, that is, "capable." In the case of Hety and Tono, being *sembodho* was more important than having good communication between them.

Closely linked to the ideals of harmony and self-control is the practice of silencing oneself. In general, the Javanese refuse to say anything negative. Rather, a Javanese will express what she or he is feeling by means of certain symbolic attitudes or behaviors, which someone from the same class will probably be able to interpret correctly.

Another Javanese ideal, especially in the *priyayi* class, is self-respect, which means the ability to carry out all duties in accordance with the social order. Self-respect is so important that sometimes, in spite of the desire for harmony, open conflict may occur.

What has bearing in this case is that according to Javanese tradition, the position of husband as head of the family is higher than that of the wife. He ought to be the educated one and the major breadwinner so that he can better carry out his role as decision maker for the family. But it is clear that Tono doesn't meet this expectation in his relationship with Hety. Therefore, as a Javanese, his self-respect is threatened because he feels incapable of playing his part in the social order. He may feel the loss of self-respect more than loss of property or other material possessions.

The Economic Picture

To understand the economic situation influencing Hety and Tono, it is helpful to remember that the Indonesian economy about the time of the attempted army coup against the government in September 1965 had almost entirely collapsed. Thus, Hety and Tono's move outside Java was not based on idealism or feminism but on economic factors—one could earn a bigger salary by working outside Java. Hety's larger salary later became a point of tension in their relationship.

When Hety and the children returned to Java, there was a major change in her economic situation because without a job, Hety had to resort to her savings. She refused to become a burden on Tono's parents because they were no better off than anyone else after the crisis of 1965.

Traditionally the man is the head of the household and the woman performs the necessary household chores, as in this scene on the island of Rote.

The Role of the Church

In the years that Tono sought to continue his study outside the country, there were not yet a lot of highly trained professionals in the church. Tono, who understood the situation, promised to dedicate himself to church work after his graduate study. The church apparently agreed to this promise but refused to support Tono's wife and children because in gaining a scholarship outside church channels, he had not given due respect to the church hierarchy. Apparently the church wished to be in control of who could pursue further study. It seemed to care more for political and organizational concerns than for what it actually needed in order to grow. Once Tono finished his studies and returned to his church, the church seemed to forget its earlier stingy attitude.

Family Concerns

The birth of children introduced a new dynamic in Tono and Hety's relationship. The children strengthened Hety's traditional role as a mother. She probably felt caught between the desire to be a good mother and the feeling that children were a burden. The absence of birth control options creates a difficult situation for women in general because their burden is generally increased with the birth of each additional child. Hety was forced to relinquish her career for the sake of her children.

Tono's family background also affected this case. In Javanese tradition, a male child has responsibility for his younger siblings and older sisters if his father dies or can no longer care for the family. That was what happened with Tono. After his father's death, his family demanded his return to Indonesia to help them. Hety urged Tono to continue his studies, but because she understood his family's need, she proposed that they send home money that they both earned. In that way they could fulfill both familial duties and their own aspirations.

Another family influence was the attitude of Hety's mother that Tono's lack of participation in domestic work meant a kind of slavery for her daughter. Possibly Hety's mother was progressive and already aware of the rights and responsibilities of men and women. Or she might have experienced a situation similar to Hety's and was unwilling for her daughter to suffer as she had. Either way, her attitude affected Hety. Even though she defended her husband to her mother, Hety's feelings at the end suggest that she secretly agreed with her mother.

Individual Concerns

It is evident that Tono and Hety did not follow a strictly traditional pattern. Their educational levels at the beginning are the same, Tono follows Hety outside Java, and Hety is initially the primary breadwinner. Perhaps these differences from the norm can be attributed to the fact that both came from Christian families.

Nevertheless, the traditions in which Tono was raised still have a heavy hand on him. As head of the family, he still determined the direction to steer the family *biduk* (river boat), he didn't want to be number two in the family. He wanted to be a rudder like any other traditional Javanese husband. He couldn't meet society's expectations of him because from the outset of his marriage, Hety's job gave her both more money and more prestige than he had. Tono conveyed his dissatisfaction in a truly Javanese manner, namely by silencing himself, that is, not talking about it. He often left home for other commitments so that there was no time left to help Hety.

Nevertheless, the threat to Tono's self-respect had a positive aspect. Because he felt challenged, he achieved some degree of social success quickly. When he had the chance to return to school, he studied energetically and finished his studies quickly. His academic success renewed his sense of self-esteem, which enabled him to return to Indonesia determined to fulfill his promise to his family.

Hety can be seen as an ambitious, courageous, and self-sufficient woman. Her ambition is not for herself but for her husband, whom she encourages to advance in his studies. It is also apparent that she experiences conflict between her desire to pursue her career and her desire to be a good mother. She suffers, but in accordance with Javanese tradition, she wants to safeguard harmony by remaining silent. After her child dies, her conflict of desires flames into anger toward her husband and God. At this peak crisis in her life, Hety is in need of help.

Interpretation: A Christian Understanding of Hety and Tono

Hety is the primary focus in interpreting this case first because the case is Hety's story and second because the final question is hers. For Christians, a key to understanding Hety is to understand the theological issues in the case, namely the tension between individual justice and the Christian call to be a faithful and willing servant. May a servant struggle for justice for himself or herself? Or must a servant always sacrifice for others? Can a balance between justice and serving others be found? We can address these questions by means of a dialogue between Hety's working theology—her views about God, faith, herself, the world around her—and the wider Christian tradition.

Hety's Theology

Hety's final question ("What was all my sacrifice for?") reveals a theological assumption behind it. Hety's suffering is the opportunity to examine the cause of evil, but she didn't ask, "Why does suffering exist?" or "Why must I suffer?" Rather she asks, "What was all *my sacrifice* for?" This question indicates how closely she relates her suffering to her relations to Tono and to God. She experiences herself as a servant who sacrificed a great deal in order to serve her husband and children well. Undoubtedly she suffered when she tried to adjust herself to a subservient, often burdensome role.

Hety's suffering can be better understood through a brief discussion about identity. Hety has two identities, a social, public identity determined by prevailing values and custom, and an inner, private one that she keeps hidden. When an individual complains, "No one understands me," it is usually because his or her private identity is so different from the mask he or she wears in public. For example, a mother is expected by society always to be willing and able to guide her children and create a strong and peaceful family atmosphere. In reality, she way feel weak, sad, anxious, and angry. From the beginning Hety's social identity and private one were clearly in conflict. But she didn't rebel or protest. Possibly she was simply going along with Javanese social values, but possibly the church had not taught her to be critical of certain social roles. It is probably safe to say that both cultural and Christian values encouraged her to accept silently her role to serve. The death of her first child marked a crisis in her life, so she began to protest.

Unless a covenant between two parties is mutual, the relationship is one of oppression. In her relationship to Tono, Hety sacrificed much in order to be what her culture considered a proper wife and mother. At first she sacrificed willingly so that Tono could win the success that would give him self-respect. She viewed her husband's success as recompense for all her burdens.

Similarly, in her relationship to God, Hety believed that in return for her sacrifice and suffering for children, it was only fitting that God the Father would protect them. The lives of her children were God's recompense for all her sacrifice. But the moment her child died, her recompense was snatched away. Hety's final question indicates that she feels her faithfulness to God and her husband and children was in vain. What she first felt to be appropriate behavior for a faithful servant she now viewed as injustice. This crisis created an enormous conflict for her because her identity as a servant and her social role as a mother were no longer clear. The assumptions about God that guided her in her servant role suddenly disintegrated. Her angry protests were thus directed toward her husband and God. She was no longer willing to accept her role as a wife who served her husband without mutuality, and she rejected the image of a God who took the life of her child.

Hety's image of God is limited. She does not yet imagine God as accompanying her in her suffering, ministering through solidarity with the weak. She would be helped if she could discover the meaning of Genesis 1:27. God created humanity in God's image, male and female, in the same degree without a division of responsibility that separates the domestic from the public. This account of creation does not give an unfair burden to women but rather blesses partnership.

Hety regards God and Tono as agents of injustice because they do not recognize her sacrifice. She needs a new understanding of God that will enable her to answer the question, "What was all my sacrifice for?"

It is dangerous to understand the concept of servant in "servant of God" as one who has lesser status or avoids confrontation. If understood in that way, the meaning of a servant has been distorted. As explained by the theologian Letty Russell, "Regardless of what the role of servant has come to mean in the history of church and society, in the Bible it is clearly a role of honor and responsibility to take part in God's work or service in the world" (*Human Liberation in a Feminist Perspective*, Westminster, 1974).

To understand this statement in greater depth, we can look at the meaning of servanthood and ministry according to the Bible and according to Paul Tillich.

The Tradition of the Suffering Servant

A prominent motif in the Jewish prophetic tradition that was received by the early Christian Church and probably by Jesus is the motif of the suffering servant. The Israelites used this motif in an effort to understand their situation as a nation that had experienced a lot of suffering throughout history. This motif was also a help to the early Christian community at a time when they were oppressed by Rome. In Christian tradition it is easy to understand the crucified Jesus to be the suffering servant as pictured in Isaiah 53:3–12, and the role of disciples who seek to follow the example of a servant Christ is very important. But how is the concept of "servant" to be interpreted, especially by women? It is important to remember that in the prophetic tradition the prophets always faced and tried to overcome injustice. They were not passive but active. In Isaiah 42:1 the servant "proclaims justice to the nations." A servant is one sent by God to serve the needs of others. A servant of God endures suffering not because God considers suffering good but rather, in an effort to realize justice.

Jesus is a servant of God not as a person of lesser status who remains silent in the face of injustice but as one who helps others discover their humanity and fulfill their self-identity. In the Synoptic Gospels his servitude is not a surrender to others who are stronger or more important but a weapon that opposes injustice. His ministry to "lesser" folk, serving the poor, was a criticism of both Jewish society and Jewish religion. His words and behavior seemed to threaten the Jewish leaders. Repeatedly he confronted the Pharisees and scribes. From the Gospels we see that Jesus' identity as a servant cannot be separated from his vision for justice. He was a servant who criticized injustice, not one who manifested an inferior role.

We need to be careful in understanding Hety's situation in the light of the biblical interpretation of "servant." She thought that because there was no mutuality with Tono her situation was unjust. Because the case was narrated from Hety's perspective, it is easy to blame Tono for imbalances in the relationship. But Hety is also at fault. By being a good mother to her children, she never gave Tono the opportunity to care fully for his children. It is important to note here that an oppressive relationship doesn't mean Tono oppressed Hety or that Hety oppressed Tonto but rather they were both oppressed by the roles they had accepted. Freedom from those roles does not mean freedom from the need to serve each other. Neither does it mean radically to sever oneself from all aspects of one's culture. Cutting oneself loose from unhealthy oppressive roles, not other basic cultural values, is the *freedom* to create new forms of truly mutual service.

Tillich's Theory of Motivation

Paul Tillich provides an analysis of individual motivation, including the motivation to serve, that may be helpful for addressing Hety's problems. According to Tillich (*Systematic Theology*, James Nisbet Co., 1968, vol. 3), motivation may be autonomous, rooted in the self (a man serves because he likes to); heteronomous, rooted in others (a woman serves because her boss or parents expect it); or theonomous, rooted in God (a person serves as a sign of faith).

In daily life, these three sources of motivation can intermingle to influence an individual to act in a certain way. All three kinds of motivation are involved in Hety and Tono's case. They chose to marry (autonomous motivation), but in their married life they submitted to the values of their tradition (heteronomous motivation) and they sought God's blessing on their marriage (theonomous motivation).

However, when it comes to their roles as man and woman and a division of labor between them, the motivations are unbalanced. They are more driven by autonomous and heteronomous motivations. Autonomous motivation is evident when Hety alone arranges for work outside Java, decides not to live with her in-laws once Tono goes overseas, and persuades Tono to continue his graduate study overseas after his father dies. But when it comes to serving her family as a housewife, Hety is heteronomously motivated as she accommodates herself to Javanese cultural values and to church order.

The relationship between Tono and Hety went along well as long as they both were operating from the same heteronomous motivation, as when Hety followed her husband abroad and cared for their two children and the household. But once there is a difference in the source of their motivations, when Tono left Java from heteronomous motivation while Hety was acting according to autonomous motivation, tension developed.

Tono drew himself away from the house rather than confront the tension. Both Tono and Hety as Javanese were silent about their problems. If they could have shared the same theonomous motivations, they might have freed themselves from the shackles that tied them to unhealthy relationships. Had they faced their problems with the love that reflects God's unconditional love, they might have used their problems as an opportunity for personal growth.

Hety's Suffering

Suffering cannot be avoided in life and cannot be experienced without some bitterness. Hety's heart will always be scarred, but the scar needn't paralyze her. If Hety can open herself to this expanded image of God and of servitude she will be better able to allow God to use her uncertainty and distress as an opportunity to learn. Her suffering can become productive. It can be a door to the new insight that someone who has been wounded need not remain a victim but can become a helper. Hety can see that her suffering is related not only to all human suffering but also to Jesus as a suffering servant. She is not alone in her suffering. As explained by Henri Nouwen in his book *The Wounded Healer* (Image Books, 1985), a person can learn to use her private suffering as a bridge for her to relate in solidarity with the suffering of others. In this way, Hety would be able to comfort others not only with words but with a heart that has experienced the bitterness of suffering.

Hety and Tono can learn that marriage is not an unjust hierarchy of authoritarian husband and obedient wife but rather a partnership united by mutual care. Both husband and wife have the responsibility to love each other and serve each other in order to develop wholeness in accordance with God's will. Without a good relationship with God there is no guarantee that they can attain a living relationship of partners. With a theonomous motivation they will be free to serve and seek justice both in marriage and beyond it.

Action: What the Church Could Do

A pastor or elder in Hety's and Tono's church could help Hety and Tono by ministering to them directly and by extension to the congregation.

Pastoral Action with Hety and Tono

If pastoral counseling with Hety and Tono simply reinforced Javanese cultural values that place the husband above the wife, it would be unsatisfactory. Hety is not likely to accept advice that seeks only quench the fire of her rebellion. The better approach is to seek ways for her to make peace with her husband and with God. The first step is for a woman pastor or church elder to place herself in Hety's position and try to experience her sense of isolation and desolation. Such an act of solidarity is essential so that Hety does not feel alone in her despair. The person might seek to befriend Hety, not instruct her. She could point out to Hety that by taking on all the household responsibilities, she did not give her husband the opportunity to share in them and so was in conflict with the true image of God. The church person could help Hety see that she is suffering not only from her child's death but also from an inaccurate concept of servanthood and Christian ministry. She could ask Hety to take on an active pastoral role with the congregation, which also holds this inaccurate concept. Such a role would offer Hety the possibility of a new dimension in her ministry to her husband and to God.

Actually, pastoral care for Hety cannot be separated from pastoral care for Tono. Because Tono has a lot of formal education and a fragile sense of self-worth, a direct approach by a pastor or elder might offend him. Instead the person might ask him to take an active role in ministry to the congregation involving a study of gender and servanthood. Such a role would place Tono in a respected position, while at the same time it might change the congregation. Because of Tono's background, unless he does such pastoral work with the congregation, he will probably go along with the prevailing attitude to maintain harmony at all costs, even if there are new insights in his life.

Pastoral Action with the Congregation

In order to support pastoral action with both Hety and Tono, pastoral action should be extended to the congregation. To be received, such action needs to be carried out within the Javanese context, which stresses harmony; therefore open conflict must be avoided.

The first step is for the pastor to prepare the congregation with sermons and talks on the concept of ministry. This topic might be especially appropriate during Family Week (celebrated by many Indonesian churches).

The second step is for the pastor or an elder to invite women who work outside the home to a meeting to discuss the problems they face as working women. At this meeting, women would have ample opportunity to share their thoughts and experiences and air complaints.

The third step is to hold a meeting for husbands of working women to hear everything the men have to say.

The fourth step is to arrange for a dialogue among all couples where both husbands and wives earn an income or for couples where only the wife is earning an income. This meeting could take the form of a Bible study or a *sarasehan* (a traditional Javanese meeting to exchange ideas in a spirit of consensus rather than debate). Finally the congregation itself should determine what actions it might take. The following examples provide some ideas:

- Families could schedule free time for working mothers. At these times the father takes over household responsibilities. Couples could begin with two free times a month and then increase from there.
- The church could set up a preschool for the children of working mothers.
- The church could organize a cooking class for fathers (to be given in a relaxed setting).

Pastoral action within a congregation could eventually be extended to regional and even national levels.

Another form of pastoral action with the congregation is marriage encounter. This is a popular three-day retreat that began in the Catholic Church in Java and has spread to other denominations. Each retreat is lead by a priest or pastor with some expertise in marriage counseling along with two couples willing to discuss openly their relationships. At some point the husbands and wives participating are separated and given writing assignments. Then they exchange what they have written as one way to express their feelings for each other.

Postscript

In the years since this case study was written, Indonesian churches have absorbed some of the lessons of Hety's struggle and that of millions of women like her. Dialogue on the roles of women and men in home and church has become a regular aspect of the church's ministry. Within the middle class, the right of a woman to her own career is generally recognized, although in practice she is still expected to adapt to the demands of her husband's work. The number of women pastors has continued to rise steadily, and women now comprise fully half of the seminary students. Although women are still rare in leadership positions, they are becoming much more vocal and less patient with male dominance. Such changes are perhaps as much owing to broader cultural change as to the efforts of the church.

As for Hety and Tono, they are still married. Tono has become a prominent figure in Christian higher education, and Hety has had a successful career as an artist.

A Woman's Day and a Man's Day

A group of women farmers in the village of Kikilai, Alor, made the following comparison of the division of labor between men and women as recorded by Karen Campbell-Nelson.

DAILY TASKS FOR WOMEN

morning
Arise about 5:00 A.M.
Draw water from the well.
Make a fire and boil water for drinking and breakfast.
Wash pots and pans from previous night.

DAILY TASKS FOR MEN

morning
Arise about 6:30 A.M.
Eat betel nut.
Wait for Mama to cook breakfast, eat.
Prepare garden tools, sharpen machete.
Walk to gardens.

Feed the children and get them off to school.
Feed the adults and preschool children.
Wash dishes.
Bathe preschool children.
Feed the animals (pigs, chickens, goats).
Prepare supplies for the day in the gardens
Walk to gardens, 1–5 kilometers (1/2 to 3 miles)

all day

Work in the gardens: helping men clear the land, burning cuttings, planting, weeding.
Gather firewood and build fire.
Gather food from gardens and cook lunch for the men.
Return to work in the gardens.
Gather firewood and fodder for animals.

night

Return to house about 6:00 P.M., carrying firewood and fodder.
Feed the animals.
Draw enough water for drinking, cooking, and bathing.
Bathe self and small children.
Cook and eat dinner.
Put children to sleep, go to bed about 9:00 P.M.

all day

Work in the gardens.
Rest while Mama cooks lunch, eat.
Work in the gardens.

night

Return to house about 6:00 P.M., carrying any larger pieces of firewood.
Play with children, tell stories.
Wait for Mama to cook dinner, eat.
Sleep about 9:00 P.M.

He's smoking a cigarette, she's carrying a load. Is this what God meant by "partnership" (Gen. 2:18)?

Chapter 6

Ties That Bind a Timorese Church

To speak of the church in Indonesia it might be best to begin by removing a few misconceptions. First, churches in former colonial areas are often referred to as "new" or "younger" churches in contrast to the "older" churches of Europe and North America. While this may be true in the case of Europe, North Americans should speak with caution here: the Christian presence in Indonesia is more than four centuries old. The first Protestant congregation in Timor was formed in 1614, six years before the Pilgrims landed at Plymouth Rock, and German missionaries were establishing churches in North Sumatra at about the time they were doing the same thing in the American Midwest. From this standpoint, we should see the Indonesian churches as our contemporaries. The two senses in which "new" might apply is that most Indonesian churches did not become independent, self-regulating bodies until about the time of World War II, and they have a relatively higher percentage of first- and second- generation Christians.

The second common misconception is that Indonesian churches are "mission churches." Of course every church is a mission church, in that they all owe their origins to the sending out of the apostles from Jerusalem "to the ends of the earth." But if by "mission church" we mean a church that is dependent on a parent church in Europe or North America for its doctrine, polity, and finances, then Indonesian churches ceased being mission churches more than fifty years ago, when the Japanese occupation forced them to stand on their own—which they have done, for better or for worse, ever since. Of course, the self-confidence to be an independent church did not come immediately. As one church leader told me, "We were taught by the colonial experience that whoever has the money, has the mission. It has taken time to change that to 'Whoever has the faith, has the mission.'" Although there is still a substantial amount of financial aid coming in from Europe and North America, it is largely supplemental. Indonesian churches today train and pay their own pastors, build their own buildings, make their own decisions, and seek to carry out their own mission.

A third misconception concerns the role of the foreign missionary. Although there is some truth to the nineteenth-century image of the missionary tramping through the rain forest searching out remote tribes, far more often missionaries were teachers and church administrators who supervised the ministry of a much larger number of indigenous evangelists. Of the nearly sixteen hundred congregations in the Evangelical Protestant Church of Timor, for example, probably less than a hundred were founded by foreign missionaries. At present, foreign personnel are almost exclusively engaged in university-level education, rural development, and other areas that require technical expertise in short supply among the local membership. They are prohibited by law from occupying leadership positions in the churches.

In the remainder of this chapter I will give a brief overview of the history of the churches in Indonesia, followed by a case study of the origins of a single rural congregation, as told by the Timorese pastor, now retired, who played a central role in its formation.

Christian Presence in Indonesia

The Christian population of Indonesia forms a small but significant minority. From 10 to 15 percent of Indonesians identify themselves as Christian, which means between 20 and 30 million people. This percentage of Christians is among the highest in Asia, next to the Philippines with its large Catholic majority. The greatest share of membership (about 60 percent) is found among what North Americans would call mainline Protestant denominations, most of whom share a Dutch Calvinist background; the remainder are Catholics and Pentecostals. As noted in Chapter 1, the majority of Christians are found in the Outer Islands, which had been relatively untouched by Islam, Hinduism, or Buddhism by the time of the Dutch period.

The earliest Christian influence came from the Portuguese, who established missions as part of their trade empire, notably in the Moluccas, North Sulawesi, Flores, and Timor, beginning about 1520. Many of these missions were surrendered when the Dutch took over in the early 1600s. The Dutch did not encourage evangelization by anyone, Catholic or Protestant, and there followed a long period of Christian stagnation. During the liberalizing period of the 1800s, the Catholic Church experienced slow but steady growth through its ministry of health care and education. After 1900 a number of missionary congregations and orders became active, and they prepared the way for the establishment of an Indonesian hierarchy in 1961.

The Protestant presence began with the sending of "comforters of the sick" on Dutch merchant ships headed for the Indies. When the Dutch took over the islands from the Portuguese, they applied the old European policy of *cuius regio, eius religio*. Each area of the archipelago was assumed to follow the religion of its ruler. Thus those areas that were already Islamic, Hindu, or Buddhist remained so. Only in the Outer Islands were there large groups of people who had not accepted one of the world religions, and it was among these people that Christianity eventually took root.

The first Protestant congregations were formed to serve the Dutch employees of the VOC, although some of their Indies servants quickly became involved. To serve the needs of this growing group, the first Malay Bible was published in 1733, translated by Melchior Leydekker.

From 1615 to 1815 the church was directly under control of the Company. When the Netherlands government took over rule of the Indies, the churches there came under the authority of the colonial governor, and the clergy were counted as civil servants. This arrangement continued rather awkwardly up until 1930, when the church was separated from the colonial government. From this colonial church, the Indische Kerk, developed four independent territorial churches, in the Moluccas, Minahasa (North Sulawesi), Timor, and western Indonesia.

Of equal significance are the churches founded by Protestant mission societies, which began to be active in the first half of the nineteenth century. Dutch, German, Swiss, and U.S. missions contributed to the diversity of Christianity in Indonesia by bringing in Lutheran, Methodist, and Anabaptist traditions in addition to the dominant Dutch Calvinism. The first missionaries to enter Indonesia from the American Board (forerunner of the United Church Board for World Ministries), Henry Lyman and Samuel Munson, were martyred in North Sumatra in 1834. The area was subsequently evangelized by German Lutherans and is today the heartland of Indonesia's largest Protestant denomination, the Huria Kristen Batak Protestan.

Like their Catholic counterparts, the Protestant missions made their greatest advances through social services. In most areas of the Outer Islands, the churches founded the first schools and hospitals. Although these essential services have been gradually taken over by the government, most of the larger churches still operate a school system up through the university level, and most maintain some form of health-care ministry. More recently, the churches have played a pioneering role in community-based rural development. With the exception of many committed individual Christians, the denominations have been less effective in their witness for social justice.

The Indonesian churches today are involved in an ongoing struggle to define their identity. Given the complex mixture of historical and cultural influences at work, it is a challenging task. Consider for example the practices for the blessing of a marriage in rural churches of eastern Indonesia. Christian (Dutch) marriage practices have blended with tribal marriage traditions and kinship structures to produce a unique local church tradition. At various stages of the marriage process, an exchange of bride-price and betel nut takes place, in traditional tribal dress and wit-

A local Methodist congregation in Sumatra runs a fish farm in Lake Toba in partnership with the United Methodist Church.

nessed by the minister. The minister then dons a Dutch-style clerical gown, and the bride and bridegroom change into Western dress (including a white wedding gown) for the church wedding. The minister preaches a sermon, probably from Ephesians 5:21–33 (first-century Mediterranean context) and the bridal pair cut the wedding cake (originally a Roman custom). At the wedding party, gongs and traditional dancing may mix with tapes of disco (African American) or country and western (Anglo American) music. The next day they may all change back into traditional clothing for the bride to be received into her husband's household, according to tribal custom.

This sort of hybrid growth is found at virtually every level of the church's life. It is a source of some confusion but also of much creativity. Indonesian churches are engaged in interfaith dialogue with the Muslim majority and in ecumenical dialogue both with their fellow Indonesian Christians and in regional and global ecumenical bodies. On one hand they seek to make their contribution to Indonesia's ongoing struggle for national unity, while on the other hand they are concerned to preserve the cultural identity of the many ethnic groups they serve. They strive to be loyal to their respective denominational traditions while at the same time developing a contextual theology that draws on the wisdom of local traditions. One could scarcely design a richer field for theological reflection.

The following case study grows out of this struggle for Christian identity. In 1989 the Evangelical Christian Church of Timor (hereafter called by its Indonesian acronym, GMIT) held a workshop on Sources of the Church's Identity. The workshop included a session of storytelling in which church elders related the "myths of origin" of the churches in their areas. The following is one such story, adapted from *Mengupayakan Misi Gereja Yang Kontekstual,* ed. J. Campbell-Nelson, B. Souk, and S. Suleeman (Persetia, 1995).

A Fire on the Mountain:
The Story of a Congregation

Reverend Manu was the son of a lay preacher from the mountains of Timor. As a boy, he followed his father in his duties, carrying the large pulpit Bible from village to village. Through his father's efforts at evangelism, most of the tribal groups in his area had been converted to Christianity, including the Oemana clan, which had been royalty in the traditional political system. The Oemana clan lived on a mountain that was considered sacred, the home of the local divinity. One day while following his father up this mountain, in a fit of anger and exhaustion, Manu threw away the heavy Bible he had been carrying.

After his father's death in 1948, a span of eight years elapsed during which Manu went to theological school and became a minister. When he returned to fill the pastoral vacancy left by his father, he found that the Oemana clan had reverted to their ancestral religion.

In 1963 a strange event occurred. The Oemana clan had seen a pillar of fire on the mountain every night for more than a month. Finally they asked Reverend Manu to come and see it and tell them what it meant. He told them, "This is a sign of God's wrath. This fire will consume you if you don't repent." He then invited them to pray, and after they had done so, the fire disappeared. Nevertheless, the head of the clan was not willing to return to Christianity. Two weeks later, a large stone rolled down the mountain and crushed the patriarch's house, narrowly missing him. He immediately went to Reverend Manu and asked if he might return to Christianity, along with all of his clan.

Some twenty years later, a car carrying members of the GMIT Synod staff approached that same mountain at night, in bad weather. While climbing the mountain, the car stalled, slipped backwards, and teetered on the edge of a precipice. If it fell, all would be killed. One of the passengers called members of the Oemana clan, and together they pulled the car to safety. The next morning clan members gathered together with Reverend Manu and performed a *naketi,* the Timorese ritual confession of sin. They asked forgiveness for their stubbornness in rejecting Christ so many years ago, and they confessed that in that place there had occurred a battle of supernatural powers and Christ had been victorious. Privately, Reverend Manu held a *naketi* of his own. He confessed that all this had happened because as a boy he had thrown away the Bible in that place.

Analysis and Interpretation: Understanding GMIT

In the lively discussion that followed the telling of this story, several themes emerged that reveal a good deal about GMIT's distinctive identity.

A Sense of Place

First we should note the role of geography. GMIT's territory is composed of mostly mountainous islands, a fact that has presented chronic communication problems, both in maintaining unity as a synod and in providing ministry for more than a thousand isolated village congregations. The heroes of GMIT's early history were, like Reverend Manu's father, praised less for the quality of their sermons than for the strength of their legs. Even today, some pastors must walk twenty to thirty kilometers (fifteen to twenty miles) over mountainous terrain to reach outlying congregations. Remote villages may be visited by a pastor but once or twice a year. The practical consequences of GMIT's geography include a high degree of pluralism and variations in local practice, as congregations are left for long periods of time to develop on their own. Other consequences are widely varying standards of ministry and a heavy emphasis on lay ministry. Rural pastors take on the role of a bishop, serving less as pastor and more as overseer and administrator of sacraments.

Even more significant for GMIT's context is the fact that geography, or rather the land itself, has a clear religious meaning. Almost all village names in Timor reflect a local landmark—usually a rock or water source, which the indigenous religion held to be sacred; people believed there to be a special relationship between themselves and their holy rock or spring. To some extent GMIT continues to be haunted by these spirits of place. The story occurred on a sacred mountain where decisive confrontations between the Christian God and the mountain spirit took place. The people believed that the automobile accident was due to the influence of the mountain spirit. The Oemana clan were called locally by the name of the mountain. It was their mountain and their spirit. So they had to be the ones to pull the car off the edge of the cliff.

Even though indigenous religion has almost everywhere been replaced by Christianity, this strong sense of place continues to be very much a part of GMIT's identity. GMIT is indeed a territorial church, bound by its constitution to form no congregations outside the province. But more than that, the presence of the church standing among the holy places of the ancestors has a unique confessional quality. In some cases, local holy places have even been "baptized" with biblical names such as Bethlehem Springs or Jerusalem Rock; a boat-shaped rock has even been linked with Noah's ark in local myth. There is a feeling that the land and its people have been claimed by God from the powers that once ruled them, and the people respond: this is our place, this is our church.

Belief in the Supernatural

A second theme that emerges in the story is a continuing belief in the supernatural. When the Oemana clan saw the pillar of fire, no question was raised as to a natural explanation, such as volcanic activity. They simply assumed the fire was a supernatural sign; the only question was how to interpret it. Likewise the auto accident was not attributed to a careless driver or a slippery road. The jealous mountain spirit was clearly trying to destroy the emissaries of Christ. This belief in the supernatural is almost universal in GMIT, especially in rural congregations. The strength of this belief came to the surface during the period of revivals in the mid-1960s, when there were reports of water turned to wine and people raised from the dead. While many GMIT members are now skeptical of the excessive claims of that period, such claims reveal an underlying worldview that is still very much in force. As a guide to life, it goes something like this: The world is inhabited by many "powers and principalities," and the power of God is only the greatest among them. The powers can be manipulated to some extent by magic (for example, some Alorese are said to be able to fly), but this is ultimately dangerous. The chief motive for religious activity is to seek the power of God as protection from these other powers. Conversely, there is no protection from the power of God other than to do God's will. If we do not do God's will, God's anger will be revealed in the form of accidents, sickness, and natural disasters. God's anger can be calmed, however, by sacrifice and the confession of sin.

Is this point of view Christian? The question is not easily answered. Within the Judeo-Christian tradition it seems closest to the pronouncement in Deuteronomy that obedience equals life and disobedience equals death. The point of view I have outlined above is not in accordance with GMIT's own confessional statements, but few who know GMIT well would deny that it represents the practical beliefs of a large portion of its members. Neither Reverend Manu nor the Oemana clan formulated their theology as explicitly as I have done here. It took shape in their own experience, in a complex interaction between personal and public events, and between indigenous religion and the preaching of the gospel. Reverend Manu's private "rejection" of God's Word as a boy parallels the Oemanas' public rejection of Christianity. He understands them so well because he feels the same struggle in his own heart.

Most Westerners would be a bit skeptical of this story, which is easy from a distance of several thousand miles. But question Reverend Manu or the Oemanas about the truth of the story, and you will sooner or later bump up against the firm assertion, "I saw the fire on the mountain." For them, it was a realistic sign of God's anger. Subsequent events (the rock crushing the chief's house, the car accident) only confirmed and strengthened their belief.

The theological possibilities that follow from an acceptance of the supernatural are, needless to say, quite different from those that follow from a rational, scientific worldview. Those who live exclusively in one of these alternatives need not be bothered by questions raised by the other. But many of GMIT's leaders, and an increasing number of its members, hold the two points of view simultaneously. They learn about volcanic activity in school, and they learn about the spirit of the mountain at their grandmother's knee. They don't believe in ghosts but are afraid of the dark. The tension this situation produces and the problems it raises for how the Christian faith is to be understood and proclaimed are a significant point of stress in the church's theological identity.

Doing Theology by Telling Stories

A third theme in the story of fire on the mountain is the interweaving of local stories with biblical tales. It could be argued that the people's understanding of the "epiphany" on the mountain is simply a reflection of Timorese tribal religion, even though they call on the name of the Christian God. This may be so, but another tribal religion is at work here as well—the religion of the Hebrews. Woven throughout the story in its present form are echoes of the Exodus accounts of Israel in the wilderness. Reverend Manu is a Moses figure, casting down the tablets of the Law in frustration at the task given him and later suffering God's judgment for it. The fire on the mountain recalls both the burning bush and the pillar of fire in the wilderness. The chief of the Oemanas shows something of the stubbornness of Pharaoh, and the people themselves, like Israel, return to the golden calf while their "Moses" is away getting a theological education.

These echoes of Exodus do not appear in sequence or in a clear correspondence with the events of Reverend Manu's story. They are more like the unconscious associations in a dream. But it seems very likely that whatever happened objectively on that mountain thirty years ago has been assimilated to the Old Testament accounts of the Exodus and that these events are now seen as the Timorese equivalent of it.

This intertwining of local stories with the stories of the Judeo-Christian tradition is not unique to this one congregation. Other congregations have found their identity in Elijah's contest with the prophets of Baal on Mt. Carmel. They were convinced of the power of the Christian God when a pastor's prayers for rain were answered after those of the local priests were not (oral tradition does not preserve the memory of how many times the reverse has happened!).

When these and other examples were discussed in the workshop, the participants came to an important discovery about the style of doing theology most natural to GMIT. Without access to books on narrative theology, they simply noted that "We do theology by telling stories." GMIT exists within an oral culture, so the storytelling genre is within easy reach. But beyond this, there was a feeling that the telling of stories was a kind of protest against dogmatics. For people unequipped to follow the language of systematic theology or argue the finer points of exegesis, and especially for a people whose experience is largely passed over by the dogmatic and confessional statements of the church, stories enable them to claim the traditions of the Christian faith as their own. To the catechisms, sermons, and endless advice and exhortations of church functionaries, they answer with a story. It is their own story, and it is for them the story of the saving acts of God.

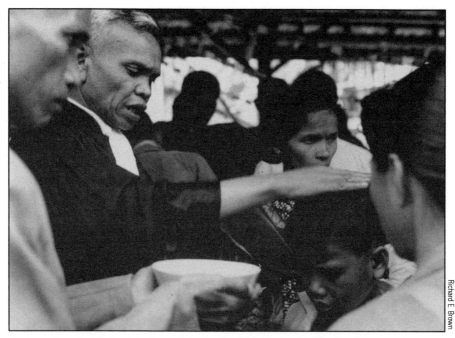

Richard E. Brown

Indonesian clergy lead their own congregations as in this baptismal scene in Sumatra .

The Role of the Family

A fourth theme of the story of Manu's congregation that reveals GMIT's identity is the role of the extended family. The Oemana clan entered Christianity, abandoned it, and finally returned, *as a family*. In Timorese, the fellowship of believers is referred to by two terms: *nonot a' knino* and *halan pap mese*. The first may be translated as "the holy family," and the second as "together at peace." The root meaning of *nonot* refers to a type of vine that is used for tying together the beams in a house. When applied to the family, it is a direct parallel to our own phrase "the ties that bind." *Nonot a' knino* appears in the Apostles' Creed where the English has "communion of saints." It carries the notion of a big extended family, "tied together" by the bonds of a common faith. It would not be too much to say that the primary meaning of faith in this context is as membership in this (holy) family. As in tribal religion, family held a sacral meaning (including veneration of the ancestors), in Timorese Christianity it was inconceivable that religion could be divorced from family allegiance. Peter Middelkoop, the pioneering missionary in much of South Central Timor, was aware of this fact. In translating Christian concepts into the Timorese language, he sought to maintain maximum continuity with the local culture. By choosing kinship as the guiding image of membership in the church, he opened the way for Timorese to enter Christianity without feeling a direct conflict with the existing family structure (except in the case of polygamy, which was never the norm, anyway).

In the story of Reverend Manu, decisions of faith are not a matter for the individual conscience; they are a family matter. Up to the present there is a strong resistance to mixed religious affiliations in Timorese families. A breach in faith is a breach in the family, and those who change religious affiliation are often disowned. Sin too is familial. It consists of actions harmful or insulting to other family members or to God and can only be cleansed by confession (*naketi*). If one family member does wrong, the whole family is held responsible: the parents of a woman who is pregnant out of wedlock may well be barred from communion; conversely the child of a couple who have not yet been married in the church will not be baptized. Salvation and the afterlife are also conceived as preserving family ties. The former custom of tattooing was intended to ensure that the person marked with the sign of the clan would be received by the departed ancestors in the afterworld, and the cross on gravestones is often believed to have a similar function. Graves are normally placed in the yard of the family home, and it is not unusual for flowers decorating the table at family worship to be afterward placed on the grave of an important ancestor. For the first generation of Timorese Christians, having pagan ancestors thus posed a problem. A salvation that cut off one's relationship to the ancestors was inconceivable. Protestantism's denial of communication with the spirits of the ancestors remains a source of tension for some GMIT members.

One of the major conclusions of the workshop was that, although GMIT's leadership has long been aware of the importance of family structures in the life of the local church, GMIT has not yet been able to incorporate this fact into its own theology and identity as a church. As one of the participants said, "We need a social concept of faith." On the level of strategy, the church has long since learned how to use traditional family power structures to its advantage. The *theological* challenge is to understand how these structures can become vehicles of God's grace, how they can be transformed inwardly by the power of Christ's love.

GMIT recognizes the social reality of a predominantly rural society in which kinship structures are still the most powerful; it also recognizes the challenge to transform these structures into a Family of God. The GMIT synod adopted this metaphor from Ephesians 2.19 as its theme for the four years 1987 to 1991, and the response from the congregations has been enthusiastic. Of the many images of the church in the New Testament, those have power that can link the new life in Christ with an experienced social reality. For GMIT, the Family of God is such an image.

Each Its Own Story

This brief picture of the origins of a single congregation is not meant to be representative of the thousands of other Indonesian communities of faith. Each has its own story, and that is precisely the point. When we are trying to understand another culture, we tend to generalize from every example we meet. Yet no list of generalizations can reveal the lived experience of a particular community. The only way to approach an understanding of a church life so rich and diverse is to listen to stories, and more stories. I think all churches are like that, insofar as they grow out of the intertwining of the life histories of many individuals, all of them, separately and together, responding to the call of faith.

Action: Reclaiming Local Traditions

One final note. Some readers may be taken aback at Reverend Manu's confrontations with the Oemana clan. We are used to criticisms of imperialistic missionaries trampling over the cherished traditions of indigenous communities—and certainly there was far too much of that, although probably less than we might imagine. But to find a Timorese taking the same approach may be even harder to swallow. Probably he was applying in his own way what he had learned from his Dutch teachers. His approach raises the issue of the relationship of the church to colonialism. That Christianity and colonialism went hand in hand is a commonplace, as well as that the missionaries carried a lot of biases in favor of their own culture. Yet there may be a legitimate theological point behind the abuses. Christianity seeks the transformation of all societies in light of the gospel of Jesus Christ. This means that all mission includes a culturally disruptive aspect, with or without colonization. The fact that missionaries were often at odds with colonial administrators simply indicates that they were competing to define the direction of cultural transformation, not that they were defenders of local culture.

Does Christian mission support colonization then? No. But it does many of the same things: it tries to bring about a change of values, challenges local customs and social structures, and seeks to influence behavior on a wide scale. This is as true of the church's mission in North America as it is in Indonesia. The question is not whether Christianity challenges culture but whether we challenge the things that *need* to be challenged in light of the gospel.

Aware that many aspects of traditional culture have been uncritically condemned by Reverend Manu's generation, a younger generation of pastors has begun the process of recovering what has been lost. Partly as a result of the workshop mentioned above, GMIT has sponsored a research project to study the rituals of tribal religion. They have begun to formulate liturgies adapted from traditional prayers for rain, the blessing of the cattle, and thanksgiving for the harvest. Prominent among the informants for this research were the head of the Oemana clan—and Reverend Manu. Nearly half the students at the seminary choose to write about local traditions for their theses. Gradually the tribal religions are beginning to take their place as a kind of Old Testament, in creative dialogue with the New.

The Gospel According to the Pig

A German missionary in Sumatra once wrote home saying that the lowly pig had proven to be a most effective evangelist. For many of the indigenous peoples of Indonesia, the pig plays an important role as the animal of sacrifice in local religious tradition. It is the animal of celebration for weddings, funerals, and peace-making ceremonies. Thus, when Muslims tried to convert these people to Islam, they were aghast to learn that they would have to give up eating pork. They wanted nothing to do with Islam. Later, when Christian missionaries arrived, the people asked them, "What is the Christian teaching about pigs?" When told that there was no Christian taboo against pork, the local people willingly embraced Christianity.

The pig continues to serve its noble function among traditional societies. Rev. Peter Tuit, a Dutch colleague of mine in Timor, once went to the remote village of Kolbano on the south coast for a lay leadership workshop. When he introduced himself to the group, there was a sudden uproar. He waited with growing apprehension as the participants carried on a heated discussion in the Timorese language. Then a local elder rose to explain in Bahasa Indonesia the nature of their debate: Kolbano was officially at war with the Netherlands. Early in this century, the colonial army had come to the village to collect taxes, and the people had revolted, killing the Dutch officers and their Javanese platoon. The Dutch had retaliated, killing many villagers and then returning to their fort in Kupang. No Dutch persons had entered the village since then. With no opportunity to restore peace with the Dutch, a state of war remained. Under the circumstances it would be impossible to continue with the workshop. Not to worry, however; the villagers had a solution. A peace ceremony was conducted between Peter Tuit, as the emissary of Queen Wilhelmina of the Netherlands, and the descendants of King Boimau of Kolbano. A well-fattened pig was slaughtered to seal the treaty, and peace was properly celebrated with a feast.

Chapter 7
Christian-Muslim Relations on Trial

In March 1997 the Indonesian minister of religious affairs, Tarmizi Taher, paid a state visit to an American seminary to inaugurate an exchange program for Indonesian religious scholars, both Christian and Muslim. With him he brought a remarkable entourage: four or five members of the executive board of the Protestant Indonesian Communion of Churches, a Catholic bishop, leaders of Muslim and Hindu-Buddhist groups, five governors, and members of the Indonesian press. Prepared speeches were distributed and a video was shown portraying Indonesia as a model for all the world of how to live in religious harmony. The conclusion of his speech is representative of the government's standard refrain:

> It is our main task, therefore, to enhance inter-religious harmony as the core element of national harmony, unity, and resilience, in the past, now, and for-ever. The sound growth of our economy, politics, and wellbeing . . . will force us to be vigilant over any threat which may disturb our national unity and integrity. . . . Therefore, it is the responsibility of every citizen of Indonesia to maintain religious harmony so that every step is really heading for the better future of the national life.

Christians may feel that the government is operating on a premise similar to that of Jeremiah: "But seek the welfare of the city where I have sent you into exile and pray to the LORD on its behalf, for in its welfare you find your welfare" (Jer. 29:7).

What Taher did not say was that even as he spoke, Muslims and Christians were killing one another in southern Kalimantan, and in the months preceding his remarks more than fifty churches in Java had been burned or otherwise destroyed by mob action, bringing the total in recent years to nearly three hundred. During the same period a number of mosques (and several Protestant churches) had been destroyed in predominantly Catholic East Timor, and several Muslims had lost their lives when local Catholics believed they had intentionally profaned the Host during Mass. These events are ruinous to Indonesia's international public relations initiative, but they do underscore the importance of Taher's remarks. On the face of it, religious strife appears to have emerged as a major threat to national stability, and the current outbreaks have left many Indonesians wondering what's going on.

Ethnic, Economic, and Political Factors in Religious Strife

I say "on the face of it" because many observers do not believe that religion is at the root of the problem. Ethnic, economic, and political factors play a significant role in each of the recent conflicts. Let's consider them one by one.

The religious map of Indonesia follows ethnic lines very closely. The great majority of Javanese are Muslims, and the fact that Java is the most populous island accounts for the position of Islam as the majority religion nationwide. Indeed, there are more Muslims in Indonesia than in all the Middle East, but they tend to be concentrated among specific ethnic groups. The precolonial trading states, notably Aceh, Sunda, and Makassar, were the first to absorb Islam, and they remain the most zealous in their practice of the faith. The people of central Java, by contrast, seem to have added Islam as the top layer to a richly textured religious life that retains the influences of previous religions: Hinduism, Buddhism, and the indigenous Javanese mysticism.

A priest conducts an odalon *ceremony every 210 days in a Hindu temple near Ubud in Bali, where Hindu influence remains strong.*

UN Photo 154857/Ray Witlin

To a lesser degree, this pairing of religion with ethnicity is true among Christians as well. South Central Timor is about 95 percent Protestant, while the island of Flores is about 98 percent Catholic. Muslims who migrate to these areas often experience a trauma at suddenly finding themselves in the religious minority. Where there is large-scale migration, as in the government-sponsored transmigration program (designed to promote national diversity and to relieve population pressures in Java, Madura, and Bali), the resentment of local people at losing their traditional lands to outsiders often appears on the surface to be a religious conflict, because the newcomers are usually Muslims and the local people of the Outer Islands are mostly Christian. This resentment was behind the unrest in Kalimantan and East Timor.

Economic factors are also clearly at work. Muslim traders along the sea lanes have honed their skills as small-scale capitalists from before the colonial period. When they move in to traditional communities that are barely on the edge of a money economy, their economic advantage is all too obvious. Even more prominent on the national level is the role of the Chinese. Many of them came to Indonesia centuries ago as traders, and their skills were well appreciated by the Dutch, who often used them as middlemen. The Javanese ruling elite followed the Dutch example to such a degree that at present, ethnic Chinese dominate the national economy. They own the largest stores and operate the factories where thousands of poor Javanese Muslims are employed at minimum wage. Since Chinese traditional religion is not one of the five officially recognized religions, many of them chose to become Christians.

Now imagine the scene on a Sunday morning in a small city in Java. Amplified organ music comes from a large and lavishly built church. The parking spaces around the church are crowded with expensive automobiles, in stark contrast to the few motorcycles and hundreds of sandals left at the door of the neighborhood mosque on Fridays. If you were a Muslim worker, and your boss, who has denied you a living wage, worships in this church, wouldn't you begin to feel resentment? This seems to have been behind at least some of the destruction of church buildings in 1996 in the Javanese cities of Surabaya, Situbondo, and Tasikmalaya.

Political factors also play a role, although they are much harder to detect. When I was in Indonesia a few months before the 1997 general elections, the political rumor mill was abuzz with talk of Operation Red Dragon and Operation Green Dragon. Red is the color of the Indonesian Democratic Party, while green stands for the Muslim-oriented United Development Party. These are the only two parties allowed to contest the government party, Golkar, in the elections. The Indonesian Democratic Party had been formed from an amalgam of Christian and liberal democratic parties, and it attracted both Christians and progressive Muslims. Operation Red Dragon refered to the government-sponsored "coup" that ousted Megawati Soekarnoputri, the daughter of Indonesia's first president, Sukarno, as leader of the party. She had become a rallying point for pro-democracy forces and critics of government corruption. She was replaced as head of the party by a government puppet. The resultant split left the party incapable of running a campaign—they managed only 2 percent of the national vote.

Operation Green Dragon, the story goes, was designed to produce a similar effect on the Muslim party but by a different tactic. There was widespread suspicion that the seemingly religious-oriented riots, so uncharacteristic of the normally tolerant Javanese, were in fact planned and fomented by government agents posing as Muslim activists. Their purpose was to raise the specter of a Muslim threat to national unity, painting Muslim activists as fanatics bent on destroying the economy, persecuting Christians, and instituting a Muslim state. Since most Javanese Muslims seem to prefer their own easy-going blend of Islam, Hinduism, Buddhism, and mysticism to the rigors of *Shariah* (Muslim religious law), they would then flee to the government party at the polls. (The same strategy has always kept Christians in line: for fear of religious persecution should a Muslim state be declared, Indonesian Christians have tended to swallow their criticisms and support the Suharto government.) As a bonus, the Chinese would be put in their place and reminded of who their political masters are. The fact that the riots in various cities followed a similar pattern, and that there were reports of large numbers of outsiders brought in by trucks for the occasion, gives some credence to this rumor. The rioters' targets reveal their mixed motives: in the town of Tasikmalaya, while 5 churches were destroyed, so were 18 police stations, 67 stores, 6 automobile dealers, 20 small factories, and 114 cars, vans, and trucks.

Perhaps the most telling argument in favor of this scenario is that it fits with Suharto's general strategy of managing the political role of Islam. In general, he has followed the Dutch tactic of promoting Islam as a religious and cultural force while eliminating it from direct political involvement. But in the late 1980s, Suharto's relationship with the military was at an all-time low. Officers were resentful of the economic privileges given the Suharto children and their allies, and of the promotion of Suharto cronies in the military over more experienced and better-qualified officers. In search of a counterweight against the military, Suharto turned to Islam. After a long reputation as a tepid, Javanese-style Muslim, he suddenly "got religion," went on the obligatory pilgrimage to Mecca, and began publicly promoting Islamic causes. But in 1997, as he faced an election in which the resentment of poor and middle-class Muslims against the government threatened to erode his power, he may have thrown his weight in the other direction by orchestrating the subversion of the Muslim party. Or so the story goes.

At the height of the riots, religious leaders came forward in an effort to restore peace. Abdulrahman Wahid, the head of Indonesia's largest Muslim group, the Nahdlatul Ulama (more than 20 million members), took the extraordinary step of publicly apologizing to Christians and asking their forgiveness for the acts of his co-religionists. Christians and Muslims in affected areas formed peace committees.

Muslim school girls, veiled according to Muslim tradition, visit the great Buddhist temple of Borobudur.

Apparently going directly to the political heart of the matter, the Catholic Bishops' Conference, again in a highly unusual direct political statement, sent out a pastoral letter saying that it would be within the rights of the Christian conscience to boycott the elections.

As the elections neared, it seemed that religious harmony was again on the mend but not quite as the government had expected. While the government had wanted to paint itself as the guarantor of peace against the threat of religious chaos, some Christians and Muslims came to agree that the heavy hand of the government was itself the problem, one that would require them to work together to overcome.

Part of this process is reflected in the speech that will make up the remainder of this chapter. The context of the speech is as important as its content. Following the destruction of churches in Java, young people in the predominantly Christian island of Timor turned their thoughts to revenge. Tensions ran high, and the local Muslim minority were in fear for their safety. There was talk of burning mosques and attacking Muslim-owned businesses. In response to this dangerous situation, a consultation was arranged in Kupang, the provincial capital of West Timor. Students from the local Protestant university met together with those from the much smaller Muslim university. The following material is adapted from the speech they heard from Andreas Yewangoe, rector of Artha Wacana Christian University, and a prominent Indonesian theologian.

PROMOTING RELIGIOUS HARMONY FOR THE STRENGTHENING OF NATIONAL UNITY

From the time that Indonesia proclaimed its independence and took its place among the nations, it was clear that Indonesia would be a pluralistic society, both ethnically and religiously.

Pluralism: Weakness and Strength

Diversity can be a powerful disintegrative force if it is not handled with care. The potential for fragmentation is especially strong if the religious communities insist on the exclusive truth of their own traditions. Of course this doesn't mean that we have to deny or regard as relative the truth of our own faith—only that we must not force other religious groups to accept the truth of our own. Aware of this need for mutual respect, since Indonesian independence we have spoken of the nation as a great family. In a family, it is not appropriate to put people in boxes according to their religion or ethnicity. This is what is meant when we say that we do not recognize "majorities" and "minorities." Of course we can calculate majorities and minorities numerically, but in the process of making decisions together, the idea of proportionality is no longer relevant. As in a family, any decision must meet the needs of every member.

Despite its disintegrative potential, pluralism can also be a great strength for the advancement of our nation. With such ethnic, cultural, and religious diversity, we can learn a great deal from one another. Adherents of one religion can learn much from adherents of another both in their daily lives and in the practice of their faith. Kenneth Cragg, an Anglican bishop from England and a well-known student of Islam, once asked, "What is it that you think of when you hear the call to prayer from the tower of a mosque? If you are honest with yourself, is it not also a call to you to lift up your prayers to God?" Cragg is saying that the spirituality of believers in one religion can be an encouragement to the spirituality of believers in another faith.

Learning from one another is nothing new in the relations among religions. When Islam entered Europe in its early stages, Muslims studied Greek philosophy (Socrates, Plato, and Aristotle) and even translated it into Arabic. In time, these Arabic translations became the basis for a recovery of these texts in the European languages, which gave impetus to the European Renaissance. Such give and take continues to the present day. As of 1996, the number of mosques built in the Netherlands had reached 100, while the Islamic population of that country had grown to 600,000. Of course the majority of these people were immigrants from Morocco, Turkey, and Surinam, but by the second and third generations they have become truly integrated into the nation of the Netherlands. The language they use is Dutch, and they have absorbed the democratic principles of the Dutch. Conversely, the Dutch learn much from these people about the importance of religious faith, especially in their own highly secular climate.

What can we learn from these developments? What stands out most is that the religions are in essence universal, in the sense that they cannot be limited to a particular nation or ethnic group. Each of them appeals to all of humanity, and they are available to all of humanity. That means that to declare a certain geographic area to be "free" from other religions (as was done recently in several districts) is a contradiction of the essential universality of the religions themselves. The simple logic of our situation is this: since there is more than one religion that offers a universal call to faith, in principle we will always find ourselves in a situation of religious pluralism.

Proclamation and the Three Harmonies

To say this is to touch upon one of the most important aspects of our religions: proclamation (evangelism for Christians, *dakwa* for Muslims). Proclamation is an essential part of our religions—without it, it is impossible to imagine how either Islam or Christianity could have come to Indonesia. What we must observe in our current situation is not that there should be no evangelism or *dakwa* (as some interpret the government's position against proselytizing), but that it must always be done with courtesy and respect. We must never force our faith upon someone who doesn't want to hear it. According to Christian conviction, the gospel is "Good News," but we can turn it into "Bad News" by aggressive and arrogant evangelizing.

In an effort to avoid unnecessary conflict, the government has promoted something called the Three Harmonies: harmony between religious communions, harmony within religious communions, and harmony between religious communions and the government. Of course this formulation is not a theological but rather a political one. Even though we have had this policy for a long time, it has not prevented religious conflict. Among Christians, we can note the conflict within the Batak Protestant Church (HKBP), which still continues even though the government has recognized one of the contending parties as the legitimate representative of the church.

More recently, riots in Surabaya, Situbondo, Tasikmalaya, and Rengasdengklok have followed one after another. Even though these disturbances cannot be labeled religious conflicts at heart, they have taken on a religious aspect. Perhaps it is true that the riots were caused by social inequalities. But why then were the houses of worship of one group (Christians) targeted when the initial problem was internal to another group (Muslims)? (Crowds were angry when a man who was considered a heretic was given too light a prison sentence by the district court.) At the very least we would have to question what sort of religious leadership has created a climate in which the anger of the people is so easily redirected toward a religious group that had no relationship to the problem. René Girard, a French literary critic, has written of the scapegoat mechanism: a victim is often required before the people are "satisfied." He means that when a society is in crisis, it needs to have a clear public symbol that can be identified as the source of the problem. In ancient religious rituals the people sacrificed an animal to obtain salvation. According to the traditions of Israel, two goats were provided. One was sacrificed as an offering for the forgiveness of sins. The other was allowed to live, but the sins of Israel were symbolically placed upon its back and it was driven into the desert. It took away the sins of Israel, and the people were restored to favor with God. Life could return to normal, because the crisis had passed. This ritual was repeated every year.

Is it possible that the scapegoat mechanism is at work in Indonesian society today? Usually it is those who are considered minorities who are chosen as scapegoats. This is one of the ways that religion can be misused. Aloysius Pieris, a Catholic theologian from Sri Lanka, says that religion is basically ambiguous. Religion can both free and enslave. In its liberative aspect, it can move individuals and societies toward greater peace and justice. In its enslaving aspect, it appears as dogmatic and fanatical. This potential for oppression is easily manipulated by those in power for their own interests. Demagogues can use the religious sentiments of the people to convince them that they are endangered by another religious group. In Indonesia, for example, we still encounter accusations of subversive plans to "Christianize" or "Islamize" our society. If this situation continues, then religion, which ought to be a force for renewal, will place us in destructive conflict. Religion then becomes an ideology, a false image of itself.

How can we avoid religious conflict in our society? There is no way but to learn to live together in harmony. It has been said over and again by our leaders that religious harmony is a prerequisite for national development. The history of other nations has proven that extended religious conflict can destroy a society; we have only to look to the former Yugoslavia, Ireland, and Sri Lanka for examples.

For Indonesians, religious harmony is nothing new. It has been a highly regarded social value since at least the middle of the first millennium (from the time of the kingdoms of Mataram and Majapahit, when Hinduism and Buddhism thrived side by side). Even today, our Constitution states that the government must guarantee a harmonious social environment in which every citizen may practice his or her religion. Our national motto, *Bhineka Tunggal Ika* ("Unity in Diversity"), is an expression of our national consciousness and our deepest feeling as a people of the need for harmony. People at the grassroots level express this feeling in their daily lives. In the villages, people of different religions may be found in the same family. Among the Bataks, there are "Nasutions" who are Christian and "Nasutions" who are Muslims, yet they are still one clan, and they remain united in their cultural traditions. The same can be found in the Moluccas and in Timor.

A Poll on Harmony

In a public opinion survey carried out in December 1996 by the Center for the Study of Development and Democracy in the three largest cities (Jakarta, Surabaya, and Medan), the following results were reported:

- The level of religious harmony in daily life in these cities was quite high. Most of the respondents said that religion did not play a role in relations among neighbors (64.3%), and that they were not bothered if their neighbors were of a different faith (88.8%). At the same time, 97% said that they would be concerned or offer help if a neighbor of a different faith were in distress. 70.6% felt that religion was not a factor in forming friendships, and 84.4% experienced no frictions in the workplace due to religious differences. Furthermore, 66.7% felt that only ability and not religious affiliation should be considered in hiring practices.
- Mutual observance of religious holidays, whether directly or through greeting cards, was practiced by 63.2% of respondents. 95.5% were pleased or considered it normal to receive holiday greetings from acquaintances of different faiths. An even higher degree of tolerance was expressed by those who supported attendance at worship services of another religion (38.8%).
- The respondents themselves confirmed the general conclusion drawn from this study, that there is a high level of religious harmony in contemporary Indonesian society. 86.8% rated it as "high" or "very high". Factors most often cited for contributing to religious harmony were: "the people's own awareness" (48.5%), "religious teaching" (35.2%), and the influence of the government (12.5%). Most felt that this atmosphere of harmony would be maintained or improved in the future (71.9%).

Although the findings of this poll are subject to a degree of error, as are all such polls, it is nonetheless the most objective measure we have at present. In light of these findings, it is all the more surprising when we encounter news stories of certain towns and villages being closed to members of minority religions, or of landlords refusing to rent to people not of the "right" religion. Perhaps these are merely isolated cases, but they deserve our attention, for they may reveal other forces at work in shaping people's attitudes.

A Christian View of Harmony

Of course religious harmony is not simply a matter of conduct in daily life; it is itself an expression of one's faith and convictions. Recently Minister of Religious Affairs Tarmizi Taher suggested that each religious group in Indonesia should produce its own "Theological Framework for Religious Harmony." The Protestant response was discussed at a consultation held in January 1997. Among those who spoke, Victor Tanya noted that both Islam and Christianity have an internal appreciation for pluralism in the ways that people worship, organize their communities, and express their beliefs. Paul called this pluralism a variety of gifts that all go into the building up of the church. In Islam the different approaches to the faith are called "pillars," all of which support the "roof" of faith, which shelters all believers. In both images, the delineation of acceptable variation within the religious community provides a "space" in which freedom and faith can grow together in a pluralistic environment. What is said within each religious tradition may also be said of the relationship among the religions of Indonesia: each can be seen as a pillar contributing to the unity of the nation.

For Christians, harmony with others is clearly a call of faith. Eka Darmaputera, a prominent pastor in Jakarta, warned against a merely "strategic" view of harmony. He noted several kinds of religious harmony that we do not want:

- Harmony as the mere absence of conflict. Conflict is not always a bad thing. After all, Jesus didn't hesitate to come into conflict with the Pharisees for the sake of the truth (Matt. 23:1–36). Harmony should never be an excuse for suppressing the truth. Rather, true harmony is found when people seek the truth together through honest dialogue—a higher truth, the truth of God.
- Harmony as a goal in itself. To the contrary, harmony is the by-product of other values. When truth is held in high esteem, when justice is done and basic human freedoms are respected, true harmony will come of itself.
- Harmony that is forced upon us by threats of the authorities. This approach can only suppress conflict; it will not produce peace, which must come from the heart.
- Harmony that hides our differences and suppresses our freedom. Trying to force everyone to be the same can only destroy harmony. According to Paul, the expression of true harmony is that "If one member suffers, all suffer together with it; if one member is honored, all rejoice together with it" (1 Cor. 12:26).

Darmaputera goes on to say that the foundation of a Christian's approach to religious harmony is the confession that we are all created and loved by the same God: "The same Lord is Lord of all and is generous to all who call on him" (Rom. 10:12). And we are all called to the same care of God's creation (Gen. 2:15).

In the current situation in Indonesia, it is essential to keep harmony and freedom in a dynamic balance. We must resist the temptation to suppress freedom for the sake of harmony. We must equally resist the temptation to demand our own rights without regard for the rights of others. Religious freedom is not merely an aspect of human rights or civil rights; it is a gift of God, given to every human being, Christians and Muslims alike. Freedom is an inherent part of our God-given capacity for faith. Therefore, if we struggle for religious freedom, it is not merely for ourselves as Christians but also for people of other faiths. Any suppression of religious freedom is a violation of the grace of God. To be consistent with their beliefs, Christians cannot simply protest when their own rights are violated but remain silent when those who suffer are of other faiths. In those areas where Christians are in the majority, they must use their relative strength not to promote their own faith at the expense of others but to defend and protect the freedom of those who are in the minority.

If these are the principles by which Protestants understand religious harmony, it is only honest to say that we do not always live by them. Yet our failings cannot obscure the simple truth: We are all made in God's image, and God is gracious to us all. If God has been good to us, why can we not be good to one another?

Betty Tankersley

In Indonesia, where harmony is a valued ideal, a Christian church exists peaceful-ly beside a Muslim mosque in Jakarta, although relations are strained in other parts of the country.

Working Toward Harmony

How can we work toward harmony in our daily lives? There is much that can be done:

We need to resume the kind of interreligious dialogue that was begun several years ago. In Christian circles, some are even going beyond dialogue to speak of partnership. A seminar of Christian youth was held in Kuala Lumpur, Malaysia, in 1980 under the theme, "Partnership with People of Other Faiths." The seminar concluded that the goal of partnership with people of other faiths is to create together a new community that is just and caring, founded on love of the neighbor, and working together to improve the quality of life for all. And rather than being pitted against one another by the forces of economic, political, and cultural change, they agreed to strive for a common understanding. They committed themselves to work together as agents of change in society, rather than accepting themselves as victims of change. Their example has much to offer Indonesian youth today.

We must learn to avoid misunderstanding the behavior and terminology of religious groups. Evangelism among Christians is not the same as "Christianizing Indonesia." Nor is the Muslim *dakwa* the same as "Islamization" of our national life and culture. Here above all we need honesty. Among some Christians, evangelism is often given the narrow meaning of adding as many new members as possible. With this attitude it is not surprising that small groups of "militant"

Christians go door-to-door forcing pamphlets on people, the contents of which are easily misunderstood. There are even those who try to force the puzzled residents to pray with them. According to the opinion poll cited above, the great majority of those surveyed in the three major cities (95.6 percent) were opposed to house-to-house visits designed to persuade people to change their religion. It is worth noting that Christians were as much opposed to this kind of "evangelism" as Muslims. At the same time, we must always allow for the freedom of conscience in which a person may come to a mature decision to embrace a religious faith other than the one in which he or she was raised. But this comes only after a deep engagement with people of other faiths.

We must avoid stereotyping other religious groups. Too often we abstract the religion from the people who believe in it, so that we are no longer relating to human beings. Marcus the Christian and Mahmud the Muslim become "the Christians" versus "the Muslims," complete with all the negative stereotypes one side has heaped upon the other. Then when there is a conflict, we no longer see the human being before us, made of flesh and blood just as we are; we see only the symbols of our own hatred. This is the fruit of many bad sermons that produce a dangerous childishness among the believers.

We must strive to prevent our religions from becoming the tools of irresponsible leaders who would use them as instruments of power. Power gained in this way is never stable or just; and religions that give themselves to be used in this way lose their integrity.

This is also a time for our religious leaders to be honest about our current situation. The Muslim social scientist Ulil Ashar-Abdalla notes that in several of the recent conflicts, houses of worship, especially churches, have become favorite targets. Many commentators have argued that the root causes of the unrest are social inequality and political instablility, but that does not explain why churches should be singled out for destruction. In both Situbondo and Tasikmalaya, he notes, the destruction has reached levels unprecedented in Indonesia's history. Muslims cannot fairly claim that this is all strictly due to social inequality.

According to Abdalla, there is a theological problem that is perhaps subconscious in the Muslim community, but it needs to be recognized if we are to prevent the further spread of violence. He calls for an honest admission that many Muslims hold a prejudice bordering on hatred of the places of worship of people of other faiths, especially Christians. This attitude is nurtured among the people by the Friday sermons in the mosques, but it is never acknowledged in the rhetoric of public officials and the Islamic elite.

Abdalla addressed his remarks to Islamic leaders in the wake of the recent violence against churches, but the same plea should be directed toward Christian leaders as well, insofar as they hold the same negative stereotypes against Muslims. Just as Christians may have difficulty building and maintaining churches in majority Muslim areas, so do Christians obstruct the building of mosques in majority Christian areas.

Stated more positively, perhaps we could say that all Indonesian religious groups face some of the same global problems: poverty, secularism, AIDS, consumerism, drugs and alcohol, social injustices. These all require cooperation among the religious groups. Our basic human problems are so great and complex that no religious group is capable of overcoming them alone.

Do university students have a unique role to play here? Of course you are a part of this nation, and its problems are your problems. It is hoped that you, as young intellectuals, will be able to see these problems critically and objectively. You are not yet contaminated by the self-interest that leads so many to abuse religion for their own ends. The idealism and the mutual understanding that you build up now will be a powerful resource as you take up positions of leadership. As you make friends, you tend not to make the usual distinctions among religious and ethnic groups; this attitude may enable you to distance yourselves from these problems and to find solutions that will benefit everyone. You have the opportunity to create interreligious and interethnic discussion groups—this is what the pioneers of Indonesian independence did when they were still students. We must learn not to close one another up in racial and ethnic boxes. Only by nurturing mutual understanding can we preserve the unity of this nation. Any other choice would lead to destruction—and that would be a tragedy!

Postscript

There were no riots in Kupang.

Overcoming Religious Prejudice, a Personal Experience

(Adapted from Emanuel Gerrit Singgih, *Reformasi dan Transformasi Pelayanan Gereja: Menyongsong Abad ke-21*, Yogyakarta: Kanisius, 1997, pp. 173–176.)

My family comes from Ujung Pandang, South Sulawesi. I was in my senior year at a Catholic high school, in 1967, when a series of attacks on churches broke out in Ujung Pandang. The day after the rioting began, I was to take my final examinations. I sat for my exams in the ruins of the school, surrounded by broken glass, bricks, and the ashes of burned textbooks and papers. We were guarded by soldiers and police. I remember that the night before, I had heard the yelling of the crowd as they destroyed the Pentecostal church in the neighborhood.

Even so, I felt no desire for revenge. Why? Because of the example of my father. He had been a nonpracticing Muslim when he met my mother, who is a Christian, and they fell in love. Because of their love, he was willing to become a

Christian; he studied the catechism and was baptized, and they were married in church. He was very serious in deepening his understanding of the faith. He was eventually chosen as an elder in the church, a position he held until his death some thirty years later.

I never heard my father criticize or belittle the Islamic faith. Every year at Idul Fitri [the holiday celebrating the end of Ramadan, the Muslim month of fasting] he visited his Muslim family and friends to pay his respects; they in turn visited us at Christmas. Although religion was often discussed, it was never in a spirit of argument, and neither side ever tried to convert the other. My father's relatives from the rural areas often spent several days at a time in our home, and on these occasions my mother took care not to have any food in the house that violated their dietary restrictions. When they prayed five times a day, we children were told to keep a respectful silence—as they did when Father prayed at the dinner table.

All of our neighbors were Muslims, and some have become lifelong friends. One in particular is a very strict Muslim, yet it was he who cried the hardest when my father died. When a local government official spoke at my father's funeral, he said that my father had faithfully carried out the mission of Jesus Christ. He is a Muslim—How could he know? Surely from his conversations with my father while he was still alive.

Both my father and I have been criticized by other Christians for not trying to convert our Muslim family and friends. They say that if we loved them, we would want to save them. This seems strange to me. Surely what is unloving is to want to befriend someone only if you can make him or her like yourself. The experience of living among Muslims has taught me to live without prejudice—without in any way diminishing my loyalty to Christ.

Chapter 8

East Timor:
Indonesia's Colony

Colonial history casts a long shadow. In the sixteenth century, when the Dutch and Portuguese were competing for control of the spice trade, one of the objects of their attention was the plentiful supply of sandalwood found on Timor, an island about the size of Massachusetts and Connecticut lying just three hundred miles north of Australia. The Dutch established their trading post at Kupang, on the western tip of the island, while the Portuguese settled in Dili, in the east. Over the next three and a half centuries, the two halves of the island followed the fortunes of their respective colonial masters. West Timor was gradually integrated into the administration of the Dutch East Indies, and it became a part of Indonesia at the time of independence with no questions asked.

East Timor became a fairly typical Portuguese colony, in which the Portuguese settled down among their hosts, intermarried, established a few enclaves of Catholicism, and administered declining trade in a spirit of benign neglect punctuated by periods of brutality. As in the west, the interior of East Timor was not considered "pacified" until 1912. It was only then that a colonial administration began to take effect throughout the island and coffee plantations were established. According to United Nations documents, as of 1960, there were just over 500 Portuguese living in East Timor, with about four times as many of mixed Portuguese-Timorese descent. An additional 3,000 Chinese merchants and 1,500 Timorese soldiers and colonial civil servants made up the remainder of that portion of the population classified in the UN document as *civilizado*. The remaining population of more than 430,000 indigenous people were classified as *não-civilizado*—"uncivilized." This term mostly meant that they preferred their own language and traditions to those of the Portuguese, and pursuit of their traditional shifting cultivation to day labor in the coffee plantations.

This great mass of "unassimilated" indigenous people is crucial to understanding subsequent events. Following a bloodless coup in Portugal in 1974, a rapid decolonization process of Portuguese colonies around the world, including East Timor, was instituted. With very little preparation, the East Timorese were suddenly faced with the task of deciding their future. The three main options were federation with Portugal, full independence, or integration with Indonesia. Political parties formed along these lines, with independence gaining the largest share of popular support. A brief civil war broke out in August and September of 1975, in which Fretilin, the independence party, emerged as victor. Early indications were that Fretilin would follow a socialist program as in Angola and Mozambique, also former Portuguese colonies. The majority of indigenous East Timorese probably had little idea of what was at stake among the competing parties; the party activists were composed mainly of urban people of mixed descent and the tiny minority of educated indigenous East Timorese. To a people oriented primarily to the clan and its hereditary lands, the ideas of federation, independence, and integration probably had only a vague meaning. Apparently they were just glad to have the Portuguese off their backs and had little sense of connection with Indonesia, so their sympathies tended toward Fretilin and independence.

Indonesia had long insisted that it had no claims on East Timor and had in fact supported calls for independence during the Sukarno era. But as Timorese independence was nearing reality, Indonesia began to lobby for integration through radio propaganda and clandestine agents, who played a role in setting up the pro-integrationist party (as one such agent boasted to me in West Timor several years ago).

In December 1975, U.S. President Gerald Ford and Secretary of State Henry Kissinger visited Jakarta. In the geopolitics of the day, the United States was still smarting from its losses in Vietnam. The prospect of a Marxist-oriented government coming to power in East Timor may have raised fears (especially in a mind like Kissinger's) of a Cuban-style threat on the rim of Indonesia. Suharto told them of his plans for East Timor, and they gave their blessing. On December 7, 1975, Indonesia invaded. Ninety-five percent of the armaments they used had been supplied by the United States.

Amnesty International estimates that up to 200,000 East Timorese—a third of the population—lost their lives in the first decade of Indonesian occupation. Some died in fighting, some from napalm dropped by U.S.-supplied Bronco aircraft, but the greatest number died from starvation due to the complete collapse of subsistence agriculture and the Indonesian strategy of evacuating the countryside to deny food and supplies to the Fretilin guerrillas. As many as 300,000 East Timorese were "resettled" in concentration camps along the coast.

Once Indonesia had established military control in the major towns, it proclaimed East Timor as its twenty-seventh province and began to pour unprecedented amounts of development aid into the area. Roads, schools, and hospitals were built, and large numbers of Indonesian civilians from other islands were brought in to run them. Transmigrants from Java were imported by the thousands to establish irrigated rice cultivation, and small traders, mostly from southern Sulawesi, followed in their wake. By the 1990s, many East Timorese feared they were becoming a minority in their own country.

During two decades of Indonesian occupation, news of East Timor has been scarce. Eight Australian journalists were executed during the invasion, and for the following years East Timor was closed to foreign journalists. By 1989, however, Indonesia felt confident enough of its control to begin letting in a few visitors from outside, and it even began to revive the tourist trade. East Timorese had begun to despair of any meaningful international support, feeling that they had been "buried alive" and forgotten. Then, on November 12, 1991, East Timor made international headlines. A demonstration at the funeral of an East Timorese youth murdered by the military turned into a bloodbath as Indonesian troops opened fire on the crowd. An estimated 250 people were killed. U.S. journalists Allen Nairn and Amy Goodman had been filming the demonstration, and their footage of the massacre was seen on television around the world. The hidden reality of Indonesia's repression was finally out in the open. With support from the European Union, the United Nations renewed its efforts, and Indonesia was reluctantly persuaded to resume talks with Portugal regarding the status of East Timor.

Much as the annexation has cost Indonesia in terms of foreign policy problems, military losses, and development aid, it has not been without its rewards. The coffee plantations have become a monopoly of the military, which also controls most trade going in and out of the island. Combat experience in East Timor has been a boon to officers seeking promotion. But perhaps of greatest potential interest are the oil reserves offshore in the Timor Straits. This underwater lake of petroleum is estimated to be the fifth largest in the world. Australia and Indonesia both lay claim to the oil, which lies along their ocean border, and have concluded a treaty to share the profits equally. If East Timor were independent, they would have to split it three ways, and East Timor would be on the way to becoming another Kuwait. The difference, of course, is that Saddam Hussein was forced out of Kuwait, while Suharto has not been made to give up what he conquered.

After more than twenty years of occupation, East Timor seems to be at an impasse. The United Nations has never recognized the annexation and has continued to sponsor talks between Portugal and Indonesia. East Timor solidarity groups have been formed in Europe and the United States, and many churches have passed resolutions in support of an act of self-determination for the East Timorese people. International support for the Timorese cause culminated in 1996 with the awarding of the Nobel Prize for Peace to two East Timorese: Roman Catholic Bishop Carlos Ximenes Belo of Dili, who has steadfastly protested the suffering of his people, and the exiled leader José Ramos Horta, who has tirelessly circled the globe trying to keep East Timor on the international agenda.

Within Indonesia itself, news of the real situation in East Timor has slowly filtered through the propaganda barrier. For years, ordinary Indonesians knew only what the government allowed to be published, and they were consequently puzzled and hurt whenever their country was criticized over its East Timor policy. As far as they knew, the great majority of Timorese were delighted to be a part of Indonesia and grateful for its development aid. Only a handful of Marxist radicals hiding in the forest posed a minor threat to security. But civil servants and transmigrants returning from the "province" told a different story. Many were shocked by the brutality of their own government and moved to pity at the suffering of the East Timorese. As one friend wrote on return from a visit there, "So many stories, all with tears and blood . . . " Such stories were confirmed by the silent witness of thousands of dead Indonesian soldiers whose sacrifice was given no public acknowledgment. At present, the growing pro-democracy movement has taken up the cause of East Timor, for the first time raising a call for self-determination from within Indonesia itself. Many feel that East Timor will only gain its freedom when the people of Indonesia gain theirs.

East Timor today seems no nearer to accepting integration with Indonesia than it was in 1975, although the nature of the resistance has changed. Whereas in the years immediately following the invasion, resistance was strong in the interior of East Timor, today perhaps only a few hundred armed guerrillas remain in the mountains as a thorn in the side of the military. The focus of resistance has shifted to a new generation of Indonesian-educated young people in the cities. Indonesia believed that by opening schools it would be able to "Indonesianize" the younger generation. What happened was quite the reverse. The propaganda in the curriculum only emphasized the difference between Indonesia's high ideals and the reality of life in East Timor. The patriotic tales of Indonesia's anti-colonial struggle against the Dutch served to inspire a similar spirit among East Timorese youth against Indonesia's colonization of *their* homeland.

At the same time, the Catholic Church has shifted from being a symbol of Portuguese colonialism to a new role as a champion of East Timorese solidarity. It is the one institution that Indonesia could not dominate directly, especially since the Vatican's refusal to recognize integration has assured the independence of Timor's bishops. Under the able leadership of Bishop Belo, himself an indigenous East Timorese, the churches have become a sanctuary, an enclave of relative freedom, and a symbol of East Timorese identity. The much smaller Protestant Church of East Timor (Gereja Kristen di Timor Timur—GKTT) has had a more difficult task in asserting its independence. Until recently, it was dominated by Indonesian pastors and Protestant generals. But a new generation of indigenous pastors has now assumed leadership. The moderator of their synod, Arlindo Marcal, at great personal risk, has made a public call for a referendum on East Timor's future and has informed the Indonesian Communion of Churches (Protestant) that from now on the East Timorese will speak for themselves.

Such is the general outline of the tragedy of East Timor. But what is it like actually to live under such circumstances? I can only offer an outsider's view. The remainder of this chapter will be taken up by selections from my journal entries from a trip through the area in 1995. I was asked to assist in translating for a delegation from the National Council of Churches of Christ USA (NCC) in January of that year, and I was glad to do so, as it gave me the opportunity to visit several of my former students who are now pastors in East Timor. Here is some of what we heard and saw. In some instances I have changed the names to protect the identities of the speakers.

A Journey Through East Timor

24 January, Dili to Los Palos

Miriam Young (an associate with the United Church Board for World Ministries) and I land at Komodo Airport in Dili an hour late. Half of the NCC delegation (the others have gone ahead) meet us at the airport and we head for Baucau (East Timor's second largest town, pop. 90,000). I am surprised to see large areas between Dili and Baucau very sparsely populated. There are very few traditional villages and rather more resettlement camps—rows of two-room shacks built with palm or aluminum siding. Many of them seem empty. Few people are in sight, fewer cattle or water buffalo. Vehicles are also rare. Only around Manututo is there much sign of normal agriculture—a good deal of irrigated rice under cultivation and more buffalo, goats, and horses than I have seen elsewhere. Throughout the trip we pass rice fields that are mostly uncultivated, probably due to limited water supply and even more limited labor supply. Almost the only tree crops we see are cocoanut trees. Some palm tapping is also evident, and I see people drinking and selling palm wine along the road.

We arrive in Baucau after dark and have supper with the pastor, Luis Pinto (a former student). We have missed the ceremonies for laying a foundation stone for a new church building, a *panti asuhan*—a dormitory for the children of rural families (priority given to children of lay preachers) who want to go to junior high or high school in the city. It is supported by Church World Service (CWS) funds [from the NCC].

As we eat, Luis tells of the atmosphere around the incidents of December 31 to January 1:

Sometime on December 31 an East Timorese is stabbed (in front of his children) by a Bugis merchant. Bugis are Indonesians from southern Sulawesi. The two men had quarreled a day or so earlier because the Timorese was selling chickens in front of the Bugis's shop, and the latter tried to chase him away. Such competition is a general source of tension: Bugis are felt to have monopolized the market stalls, and the East Timorese are forced to sell on the walkways in front. The East Timorese dies on the spot, and his children begin to cry out. The Bugis runs to take shelter with the police. As word gets around, young people begin to gather, many of them no more than children. They take gasoline and pour it around the shops and set them afire, often beating the Bugis owners, who are taken by surprise. There is no looting, only burning. Christian-owned shops are left alone. The Javanese food stalls will also be destroyed, although the Javanese are given until noon on January 1 to salvage what they can beforehand. When riot police attempt to intervene, they are stoned. When they fire warning shots, a shout goes up, "Guns are for shooting enemies, not for killing the people." The police withdraw. Although arrests are made, the police are unable or unwilling to stop the burning or to control the streets. The youth set up roadblocks and check I.D. cards. Anyone from Sulawesi is warned to get out of town, and many are beaten. The movement to exile the Bugis spreads to small fishing villages along the coast.

Luis speaks of the situation in the church: since many of the congregation are "outsiders," they are afraid to go home after the New Year's Eve service, while young people are controlling the streets. Luis is not afraid because he is East Timorese, so he escorts some of the congregation home.

The market now stands burnt-out and empty. Reports of arrests, injuries, and deaths are vague and conflicting. Bugis still in the area are sheltering at the "Base Camp"—whether this is an army facility or a construction camp is unclear.

The murderer was quickly tried and sentenced to twelve years in prison, the normal punishment for unpremeditated murder.

From Baucau we travel on to Los Palos, arriving at about 9:00. There we catch up with the rest of the group. We sleep in a guest house that has apparently been built by the police, right across the street from their headquarters. Good way to keep an eye on visitors.

25 January, Los Palos

We breakfast at the pastor's house. She is rather distant—a good hostess but nothing more. Her husband is a doctor and head of the local health department; both are from Manado. Neither of them expresses any opinions about East Timor in my presence.

Our first stop of the day is the village of Homé Baru, where a farmers' group has been supported by CWS funding and the work of an East Timorese motivator, Constantino Pinto. It is one of four or five such groups. They meet us with a traditional ritual of greeting and present each guest with scarves made by the women's weaving group, who also display their work for sale. After introductions and a prayer, we go to their gardens. Maize, peanuts, soybeans, greens, and carrots, planted in rows. Once again I note almost no cattle or buffalo. Francisco, a GKTT pastor who has been our guide on this part of the trip, tells me this is a result of the war. Some of the heaviest fighting took place in Los Palos, and the cattle were decimated along with the people.

Homé Baru (baru = "new") is baru because people were removed from the old village in the hills as part of the massive resettlement campaign that took place during and after the war. The basic strategy seems to have been that villages in the interior were forced to move to the coast and the roadsides to make them more accessible to the government—much as in other parts of the Outer Islands but with the added threat that those found in the interior would be deemed supporters of Fretilin and shot. The disruption of agriculture in this way is a major reason for the famines. In Homé, they seem to be just in the early stages of reclaiming and reconstructing their agricultural system. The farmers report that it has recently become safe to return to their old lands, and there are clear signs that a dual residence system is developing, much as one finds in Alor and parts of West Timor: a "government" house is established along the roadside and near the coast to comply with the authorities, but the people actually spend most of their time at a "garden house" in the old village site in the hills.

One of the adverse effects of the resettlement is the diminishing authority of traditional leaders. In the old villages they controlled tribal altars and land distribution. Authority over land use is very unclear in the new settlements, and the farmers indicated great uncertainty about what land was "theirs" and whether the government would allow them to keep it. Plots are divided individually but worked communally. Traditional religion was also labeled a sign of Fretilin affiliation, so as in 1965 in Indonesia during the anti-Communist purge, people were eager to disguise any evidence of allegiance to it. In this way the two main bases of traditional authority have been undermined.

This "temporary" feeling due to uncertainty about land ownership is a major hindrance to agricultural development and probably explains the lack of interest in tree crops and other perennials. Security of the food supply from one growing season to the next is the dominant concern.

During the visit we are accompanied by three plain-clothes police intelligence officers. Two, from West Timor and Java, are well-behaved. The third, claiming to be from Homé, follows us on a motorcycle from which the plates have been removed. He looks and acts like a thug and seems to know little about the local culture.

In the afternoon we visit the health clinic and *panti asuhan* (dormitory) run by the church with CWS support. The clinic is staffed by a Javanese and a German nurse, the latter supported by World Evangelization for Christ. There seems to be little clear reason for the Protestants to be operating a clinic with the larger Indonesian clinic nearby, except that the quality of human care was claimed to be better in the church's clinic than at the government facilities, and it provided medicine at subsidized prices. Perhaps it also gave medical care to those wounded in altercations with the military. The *panti asuhan*, like that in Baucau, is supervised by church members from West Timor and seems to copy models they have known from the church there.

That night there was to have been a meeting with the regent of Los Palos, but he was late returning from a meeting in Dili. The vice regent wanted to see us instead, but Arlindo (accompanying the delegation as moderator of GKTT, and a former student of mine) begged off. The reason: the regent is East Timorese, and one could have meaningful conversation with him; the vice regent is Javanese and has a reputation as a slick and devious bureaucrat. This is a pattern throughout East Timor: an indigenous figurehead in the top government position with an Indonesian as number two. Who really wields the power is open to question.

26 January, Viqueque

Returning from Los Palos, we stop again in Baucau to see the burnt-out market—the old Portuguese Mercado. The new Indonesian-built market is also in similar condition. The rubble has been cleaned up, but there is no sign of anyone returning to set up shop. Military and police presence is somewhat less evident in Baucau than in Los Palos—some East Timorese think that they are intentionally lying low. On the road south from Baucau to Viqueque, we begin to notice military outposts on the hilltops, roughly every five kilometers (two miles). Nearly all soldiers we see are armed and wearing combat gear. Some are patrolling the road on foot. We also see a number loitering in civilian clothes, trying unsuccessfully to look local. Despite the military's claim that they are there more for "development" purposes than for security, throughout the entire trip we saw a large number of troops, but none were doing any kind of physical labor or anything else that looked like work.

In Viqueque we have coffee with the pastor, Soleman Marey, and go directly to the police headquarters to be registered. Several of the police are again from West Timor, and when they find I speak Indonesian with a Kupang accent they are all smiles. A traffic policeman from West Timor (who is also a church elder) will be our "watcher" throughout the stay in Viqueque. He jokes a lot and expresses no opinions. We take our luggage to the guest house, once again across from the police station.

In the afternoon we visit briefly with a sewing class taught by Susana, the pastor's Ambonese wife, and then head for a rural congregation on the south coast. We see again the pattern of large uncultivated areas interspersed with patches of maize. Pastures are underpopulated. The houses are all very small and seem more like refugee quarters than permanent dwellings.

There are about 5,000 East Timorese Protestants in this area, most of them converted from tribal religion in the early 1970s. The lay preacher, Antonio, says that until recently his congregation was larger than its present 250, but that many have returned to their old villages in the mountains, "now that it is safe to go back." The pastor serves this area about once a year to bring the sacraments and is always received with gratitude. He is offered a military escort on these trips but always refuses—he agrees with my comment that he is safer without it. Several times he has met guerrillas but has had no trouble. When asked by CWS what their major needs are, Antonio says "tools," for agriculture, fishing, and construction. They have the skills and the resources but no tools.

We return at sunset by way of the old Viqueque harbor. The pier is gone, and less than a dozen fishing boats are in evidence. That night and the next morning we talk with Marey and his wife and a few church elders (all from other islands).

give political statements, only religious. We are dealing with people, the physical abuse of the people . . . . I am not going to be silent . . . . I can't distinguish between the political issue and the moral issue when in front of me is a human being—sometimes I must speak out strongly."

Asked if he had seen any signs of improvement after the 1991 massacre, he said simply, "No. If anything, it is getting worse."

Our next stop is the military headquarters. There we get a well-polished briefing from a very articulate officer. "Indonesia had no intentions toward East Timor until a group of East Timorese themselves asked to become part of Indonesia. They invited us to come in and put a stop to the civil war, which we did. Our mission now is one of development, since the Portuguese did nothing here for 350 years, and the people are very backward." We ask why Indonesia doesn't allow a referendum if it is so confident that the majority of East Timorese want to be part of Indonesia. "Under present conditions it would just reopen the divisions the people faced in 1974–1975. It could reignite a civil war."

Next stop is the vice governor, a Javanese retired general. He talks for almost an hour and says nothing much, other than to emphasize how backward the East Timorese are, and how Indonesia is educating them and slowly bringing them out of their primitive conditions. I know it is time to go when I suddenly feel an urge to translate with Jabberwocky: "Twas brillig, and the slithy toves did gyre and gimble in the wabe."

29 January, Departure

Our last day is a Sunday, and we go to Hosana, the largest GKTT congregation in Dili. The parking lot tells the whole story. During the first, Indonesian-language

Government officials from the city give orders to rural farmers and tribesmen in East Timor and other islands often without considering the people's welfare.

service the lot is filled with cars and motorcycles, many of them bearing government plates. The people are well dressed and well fed. During the second, Timorese-language service, the lot is empty except for the pastor's motorcycle. Everyone else comes on foot. The people are thinner, and their Sunday best is faded from many washings. We shake their hands and take our leave.

Looking down from our departing plane, I feel guilty for seeing what I've seen, like a tourist in hell.

For one who loves Indonesia as I do, this has not been an easy chapter to write. Ben Anderson, one of the finest U.S. scholars of Indonesia, expressed the same feeling when he addressed a United Nations committee on East Timor. He spoke of "a profound sadness" and called the annexation "a disservice to Indonesia." The financial and moral cost of the occupation has been immeasurable. Even judged by the self-interest of the Suharto regime, the dogged refusal to recognize this terrible mistake is an ongoing disaster. An East Timorese diaspora has carried the cause of freedom for East Timor not only to Europe, Australia, and the United States but to Indonesia itself. Hundreds, perhaps thousands, of bright and dedicated young East Timorese are bearing quiet witness to their people's suffering in the universities, offices, and factories of Java just as others are doing in the United Nations, the U.S. Congress, and the European Parliament. Their commitment and willingness to risk arrest and imprisonment has been an inspiration to their Indonesian counterparts in the struggle for democracy.

Few expect significant change while Suharto is still in power. But if the untiring struggle of the East Timorese can be supported by the United Nations, the United States, and other significant trading partners, a subsequent Indonesian government may yet be persuaded to cut its losses and give the East Timorese their right to choose their own destiny.

Conclusion

On my last trip to Java in 1997, I stopped at a Christian university to visit a friend. It was just before the national elections, and I wanted to get his reading on the current state of affairs in Indonesia. His reply was interrupted by frequent fits of coughing. He has chronic bronchitis. Born in Sulawesi, he has a Ph.D. from Edinburgh, is a prolific writer, and is dean of a theological school—and he makes $250 a month. He can't very well afford a car, so he rides his bicycle to work each day through the city traffic, thus the bronchitis. Jakarta is now the number three city in the world for pollution. Pollution has become a status symbol of sorts, much like the village people in Timor who throw biscuit wrappers in their yards as a sign for all to see that they have consumed store-bought goods.

My friend is pleased because he has just won the first round in a fight to get the government to recognize theology as a legitimate academic discipline within the national education system. At stake was the right of the theological schools to grant degrees to their graduates. It seems that government officials try to regulate every aspect of life, whether they understand it or not. We both laughed at the picture he painted of his efforts to teach "Sunday school" to a roomful of bureaucrats in Jakarta.

He was concerned about his students, however. "With all the pro-democracy demonstrations going on, they would rather be in the streets than in the classroom. I understand. I was like that myself in the '70s, but I remember how many of my friends went to jail and had their careers ruined. Now the police are watching the campuses very closely. I don't know what's going to happen."

Not unlike my friend, almost every observer of Indonesia these days concludes on a note of nervous expectation. Nervous, because the political system is showing signs of serious instability as various factions jockey for position in the waning years of Suharto's reign, and social unrest reaches a level unprecedented since the terrible upheaval of 1965. Expectant, because Indonesia has a lot going for it. To review some of the accomplishments mentioned in earlier chapters: the country has made tremendous strides in the development of its infrastructure: roads, hospitals, schools, telecommunications, and industrial capacity have more than quadrupled since 1975. Electrical generation has grown eighteenfold. The economy has grown at a rate double that of the United States for the past decade or more. And there has been a corresponding benefit to the people. Life expectancy is on the rise, literacy rates have reached nearly 85 percent, and per capita income has increased at a rate faster than inflation. Many Indonesians are justly proud of their nation's accomplishments in its brief fifty years of independence. Most of that growth has occurred under Suharto's leadership, and until recently most Indonesians seem to have been willing to put up with the attendant corruption and restrictions on their freedoms in return for the promise of a better future.

But in the last few years a widespread dissatisfaction has become apparent. The two problems most often raised by Indonesians themselves are the growing gap between rich and poor and the lack of effective democratic controls on government. Official poverty statistics put the number of poor at 26 million, but when more sophisticated quality-of-life measures are taken into account, nearly half the population live just on the edge of subsistence. At the same time, some of the world's richest people are Indonesians, chief among them President Suharto himself. In the July 28, 1997, issue of *Forbes* magazine, he was named the sixth wealthiest man in the world, with a personal fortune of $16 billion. (If the wealth of his children were added, the Suharto family would move farther up the list. In all, seven Indonesian families and individuals are listed among the *Forbes* two hundred wealthiest people in the world.)

The connection between personal wealth and political power has reached a point where "people are nauseated by it," as one friend put it. There is a growing perception that Indonesia has essentially become an oligarchy under Suharto's New Order. Direct intervention by the president to protect the economic interests of his family and friends is commonplace, and lower-level officials follow suit all the way down to the village level. A new phrase has come into use among critics of the regime: "The Satanic Trinity." It refers to the collusion among government, military, and business figures that many feel is the dominant force behind both government policy and law enforcement. The widespread manipulation by the government of the 1997 general elections to ensure the victory of its party did nothing to dispel such perceptions.

In light of such abuses it is all too easy to dismiss Indonesia as yet another developing country that has fallen into despotism for lack of democratic traditions and is being plundered by its own elite. As I hope this book has shown, the reality is much more complex than that. In many ways, I have come to think that Indonesia and the United States have much in common. The similarities begin with their respective national mottoes: *Bhinneka Tunggal Ika* translates as "Unity in

Diversity"—not too far from *E Pluribus Unum*, "From Many, One." Apropos of their mottoes, both countries continue to struggle with ethnic and racial diversity; both are committed to a pluralistic society despite the dominance of a single group (Northern European in the United States, Javanese in Indonesia). As alarmed as U.S. Christians may be when they read of church burnings in Java, it should not escape our notice that more churches have been burned in the United States in recent years (most of them with predominantly African American membership) than in Indonesia. The fact that not Muslims but fellow Christians are doing the burning here is hardly comforting. And our alarm over human-rights abuses in East Timor must always be tempered with humility as we remember U.S. atrocities in Vietnam.

Even the two major concerns raised by Indonesians in the paragraphs above have an echo in the United States. The gap between rich and poor in the United States is growing, perhaps just as fast as in Indonesia. According to figures compiled by the Share the Wealth campaign, the top 10 percent of the U.S. population own 70 percent of the nation's wealth, and the top 1 percent own 40 percent of the wealth—a rate of concentration that has doubled in the last twenty years. This is a level of economic inequality that nearly matches that of Indonesia. If Indonesia has a small but growing middle class, the United States has a large but declining one. Real wages for U.S. workers have decreased in the past twenty years even as U.S. companies have opened factories in Indonesia, often employing Indonesian workers at less than a living wage. The situation in Canada is not dissimilar.

Such correlations are no accident. Global capitalism has brought the same benefits to investors and managers in Jakarta as it has to those in New York, while at the same time throwing U.S. workers into the same labor pool as Indonesians like Sumi and Marsinah (see ch. 2). If present trends continue, U.S. workers may soon have to settle for a similar subsistence-level income in order to keep their jobs. United States-based labor organizations have apparently drawn the same conclusion. They have begun to lobby on behalf of Third World workers, on the assumption that decent wages, benefits, and protections for these workers would reduce the incentive for corporations to move the jobs overseas in the first place. Perhaps the international labor solidarity that Communists once dreamed of will finally emerge, ironically just when Marxism has officially been buried by the global victory of capitalism.

On the political front, campaign finance scandals in the United States in the last few years have raised the question of just how effective U.S. democratic institutions are in reflecting the will of the people. Americans are discovering, just as Indonesians have, that corporate interests can buy access and influence in the political process to a degree that makes a mockery of the principle of one person, one vote. As a direct consequence of the globalization of the economy, we are also witnessing the growth of global influence-peddling. The contributions of the Riady family of Indonesia (who are also on that *Forbes* list, by the way) to a U.S. presidential campaign are a case in point. When the news broke in the Indonesian press, some took a perverse comfort in the knowledge that theirs is not the only political system to be corrupted by the lure of foreign money.

Such comparisons between the United States and Indonesia suggest that we are partners in misery, and there is some truth in that. We could perhaps learn much from one another in our common quest for ethnic and racial harmony, a just economic system, and a restoration of the voice of the people in politics. I hope this book has made some contribution toward enabling North American readers to learn, not only *about*, but *from*, Indonesia. Adopting the case study approach has meant that as much as possible we have heard from Indonesians themselves about the struggles they face. Yet there are two limitations that I think must be noted by way of conclusion.

First, the problem-centered aspect of case study has meant that I have focused perhaps disproportionately on the conflicts and injustices in Indonesian life. I have spent more time in the shadows than in the light. Most of the material I have adapted from Indonesian authors was never intended to be read by "outsiders," and I fear many of my Indonesian friends would be rather unhappy to see their people's problems and weaknesses thus exposed to the scrutiny of foreigners. My apology to them is that it was done with a feeling of love and respect, which I hope has been obvious to the reader. And there are plenty of coffee table books available that display the natural beauty and cultural riches of Indonesia far better than I could do.

Second, case studies tend to focus on the unusual; after all, if there were nothing unusual, no one would have bothered to tell about it. I have intentionally avoided some of the most exotic cases that were available, however, because exoticism is a peculiar weakness of North Americans and Europeans when they encounter other cultures. Tales of cannibals, headhunters, pirates, and witch doctors have so clouded our view of Asians and Africans that we no longer see their humanity. Yes, many of the ethnic groups of the Outer Islands once practiced headhunting as a part of their rituals of warfare. Barbaric? Well, consider that the head of the enemy was treated with honor, as a kind of war memorial and a symbol that the enemy had been tamed and domesticated. Consider also that their tribal wars rarely claimed more than a handful of victims before a peace was negotiated. It took Western ingenuity to discover how to annihilate people by the thousands. So who are the barbarians?

To put the shoe on the other foot, there is a common belief in rural eastern Indonesia that Westerners were headhunters, too. I often saw children running from me in fright when they met me on a trail near a village I was entering for the first time. The story is that whenever the Dutch built a new road, school, or bridge, they would bury the head of a child in the foundation "to strengthen it." No wonder the children were afraid. I have found no record that the Dutch actually did any such thing. But if you take the time to decipher the symbol, it makes sense: roads, schools, and bridges were the means by which the outsiders gained access to the hearts and minds of the indigenous people. Send your children off to school, and they will be changed by the strange new teachings of the Dutch. Their heads will be taken, even if their bodies return to the village. By that rather ingenious logic, yes, we too are headhunters.

The real danger of exoticism is that we Westerners distance ourselves from the humanity of the other. We say, "They are not like us," with the implication that we are therefore absolved from applying the same ethical standards in our behavior to them as we do in our behavior to "our own kind." That kind of thinking is what made slavery and colonialism possible. We say, "Life is cheap in Asia." But anyone who has heard the wailing at a Timorese funeral or felt the touch of the mourners as they pressed their own tears to your cheek, would not think so. "But they are *used* to poverty," we say. "They know how to live on next to nothing." Our family once paid for medical care for a neighbor's boy who had a severe infection in his leg. The treatment saved his leg at a cost to us that amounts to less than a meal at a mediocre restaurant. When his mother came to thank us, she wept bitterly because she had been too poor to pay for the treatment herself, and she had nothing to give us in return. Who could get used to that? And if "they" know how to live simply, shouldn't we take that as a lesson to be learned from them, rather than using it as an excuse for our own bloated sense of the "necessities" of life?

The reality is that we are exotic to one another. Everywhere the tourists watch the locals and the locals watch back. Yet I hope that through the stories of this book the reader has not only gained a deeper appreciation for the diversity of human life but also a still deeper sense of our common humanity. I don't mean that merely in the sense of our growing interdependency due to global communications and a global economy. Long before the global reach of MacDonald's and Coca-Cola, before the Dutch came looking for spices, before Marco Polo heard rumors of the islands "below the winds," the principle was laid at the foundation of our religious heritage that we are all alike created in the image of God. Racism, colonialism, and nationalism have perpetually tried to set that principle aside, but it has never been entirely erased from the Christian conscience.

Finally, our common humanity is neither a fact of history nor a product of the genetic code so much as it is an act of faith. I can say it no better than in the words of our housekeeper in Timor. When a visitor was making rather too much of how our white children played so naturally with their brown neighbors, she simply shrugged her shoulders and said, "All blood is red."

Selected Books and Other Resources

Books

History and Culture

Anderson, Benedict R. O'G. *Mythology and the Tolerance of the Javanese*. Monograph series of the Modern Indonesia Project. Ithaca: Cornell University, 1965. Highly influential study of Javanese culture.

Fox, James. *Harvest of the Palm: Ecological Change in Eastern Indonesia*. Cambridge, Mass.: Harvard University Press, 1977.

Ricklefs, M. C. *A History of Modern Indonesia c. 1300 to the Present*. Bloomington: Indiana University Press, 1981.

Vlekke, B. H. M. *Nusantara: A History of Indonesia*. The Hague: van Hoeve, 1965. A thorough and readable history up to World War II.

Wertheim, W. F. *Indonesian Society in Transition*. The Hague: van Hoeve, 1956.

Contemporary Issues

Kahin, Audrey, and George Kahin. *Subversion as Foreign Policy: The Secret Eisenhower and Dulles Debacle in Indonesia*. Seattle: University of Washington Press, 1997. Thanks to the Freedom of Information Act, we now have the story on U.S. covert military intervention in Indonesia in the late 1950s.

Lubis, Mokhtar. *Indonesia: Under the Rainbow*. Singapore: Oxford University Press, 1990. A portrait of Indonesia to 1970 by a prominent Indonesian novelist.

McNeely, Jeffrey A., and Paul Spencer Wachtel. *The Soul of the Tiger*, New York: Doubleday, 1988. On the relation of animals to all aspects of southeast Asian life.

May, B. *The Indonesian Tragedy*. Boston: Routledge & Kegan Paul, 1978.

Schwarz, Adam. *A Nation in Waiting*. Boulder, Colo.: Westview, 1994.

Vatikiotis, Michael. *Indonesian Politics Under Suharto*. New York: Routledge, 1993.

Religion

Cooley, Frank. *Indonesia: Church and Society*. New York: Friendship Press, 1968. A survey of Indonesian churches.

Geertz, Clifford. *The Religion of Java*. New York: Free Press, 1959. Classic anthropological study of religion and class in Java.

Katoppo, Marianne. *Compassionate and Free: An Asian Woman's Theology*. Maryknoll, N. Y.: Orbis Books, 1980. Written from a Protestant perspective, an easy-to-read book, though now dated, that offers an introduction to theological issues for women in the Indonesian context.

Kipp, Rita Smith, and Susan Rodgers, eds. *Indonesian Religion in Transition*. Tucson: University of Arizona Press, 1987.

Literature

Beekman, E. M. *Troubled Pleasures: Dutch Colonial Literature from the East Indies, 1600–1950*. Oxford: Clarendon Press, 1996. A survey of Dutch views of Indonesia during the colonial period by the editor of a series of Dutch colonial literature in English translation.

Kartini, Raden Ajeng. *Letters of a Javanese Princess*. Trans. Agnes Symmers. New York: Knopf, 1976.

Lubis, Mokhtar. *Twilight in Djakarta*. English translation. New York: Hutchinson, 1963.

Multatuli. *Max Havelaar*. Trans. Roy Edwards. Amherst: University of Massachusetts, 1982. Nineteenth-century exposé of conditions on colonial plantations, influential in changing Dutch policy.

Toer, Pramoedya Ananta. *This Earth of Mankind*. New York: Morrow, 1991.
—. *Child of All Nations*. New York: Morrow, 1993.
—. *Footsteps*. New York: Morrow, 1995.
—. *House of Glass*. New York: Morrow, 1996.
Volumes of the Buru Quartet, depicting Javanese life under the Dutch in the early twentieth century, narrated in prison by Indonesia's preeminent dissident writer.

Roskies, David M. C. *Black Clouds over the Isle of Gods and Other Modern Indonesian Short Stories*. Armonk, N. Y.: Sharpe, 1997.

East Timor (available from ETAN, see below under organizations)

East Timor Working Group, NCCCUSA Southern Asia Office, Room 620, 475 Riverside Drive, New York, NY 10115

Carey, Peter, and G. Carter Bentley, eds. *East Timor at the Crossroads: The Forging of a Nation*. Honolulu: University of Hawaii Press, 1995.

Jardine, Matthew. *East Timor: Genocide in Paradise*. Tucson, Ariz.: Odonian Press, 1995.

Jardine, Matthew, and Constancio Pinto. *East Timor's Unfinished Struggle*. Boston: South End Press, 1996.

Taylor, John G. *Indonesia's Forgotten War: The Hidden History of East Timor*. London: Zed Books, 1991.

Magazines and Journals

Inside Indonesia. Bulletin of the Indonesia Resources and Information Programme (IRIP), from Australia. An excellent quarterly that provides in-depth coverage of contemporary social, political, cultural, economic, and religious issues. American subscriptions are US $28 annually to: Indonesia Publications, 7538 Newberry Lane, Lanham-Seabrook, MD 20706.

Indonesia. Cornell Modern Indonesia Project, Ithaca, New York. The preeminent U.S. scholarly journal on Indonesia.

Far Eastern Economic Review. GPO Box 160, Hong Kong. Also available on-line at www.feer.com. The best source for news on Southeast Asia.

Asiaweek. P.O. Box 62080, Tsat Tze Mui Post Office, Hong Kong. Also available on-line through www.pathfinder.com.

Organizations

American Indonesian Chamber of Commerce, 711 Third Ave., 17th Floor, New York, NY 10017.

Campaign for Labor Rights, 1247 E Street SE, Washington, DC 20003. Also on-line at www.compugraph.com/clr/. Active in the Nike boycott and other international labor issues.

Cultural Survival, 96 Mount Auburn Street, Cambridge, MA 02138.. Information and advocacy on rights of indigenous peoples.

East Timor Action Network (ETAN), PO Box 1182, White Plains, NY 10602. East Timor advocacy and newsletter.

Global Exchange, 2017 Mission Street #303, San Francisco, CA 941110. e-mail: gx-info@globalexchange.org; web: www.globalexchange.org. Economic advocacy and alternative travel and tours (including Indonesia).

Human Rights Watch/Asia, 1522 K Street NW, Suite 910, Washington, DC 20005. e-mail: hrwdc@hrw.org. Monitors human-rights situation in Indonesia and other Asian nations. Its responsible and well-researched reports are frequently consulted in congressional hearings. Publications: *Human Rights Watch*, 6 a year.

Indonesia Tourist Promotion Office, 3457 Wilshire Boulevard, Los Angeles 90010.

Volunteers in Asia, P.O. Box 4543, Stanford, CA 94309. e-mail: volasia@volasia.org; web: www.volasia.org. Provides placement for one-year service in Asia, including an active program in Indonesia. Many college students have gone as English teachers and development workers through this organization.

Film and Video

The Year of Living Dangerously, starring Mel Gibson. Widely available from video rental shops, a commercial film that follows a jounalist's experiences during the 1965 coup.

Riding the Tiger (Australian Broadcasting Corporation, 1993). Christine Olsen and Curtis Levy: Award-winning series, originally shown on Australian TV.

Beyond the Ring of Fire (PBS, 5 videocassettes, $99.95), Lorne and Lawrence Blair. A record of ten years' living and traveling in Bali and the eastern islands. Available from PBS.

Manufacturing Consent: Noam Chomsky and the Media (1992). Peter Wintonick and Mark Achbar. Includes comparison of media coverage on East Timor and Cambodia. Not for the fainthearted—over three hours. Available from ETAN)

Blowpipes and Bulldozers, Jeni Kendell and Paul Tait. Story of the Penan people of Borneo and their struggle to survive in the destruction of their forest habitat by logging interests. Filmed in Malaysia, but the same problem is happening on the Indonesian side of the border. Available from Bullfrog Films, Box 149, Oley PA 19547; ph. (800) 543-3764.

Arrows Against the Wind, Tracy Groome. Filmed secretly in Irian Jaya, a documentary on the rich life of two tribes, the Dani and Asmat. Also the story of their social, political, and environmental upheaval. Available from Bullfrog.

The Price of Progress, Nicholas Claxton. Investigation of three huge resettlement schemes sponsored by the World Bank, in India, Indonesia, and Brazil. Available from Bullfrog.

Not the Numbers Game. A BBC program on the role of women in development and population control. Includes a segment on Nike factories in Indonesia. Available from Bullfrog.

The Internet

Without doubt the Internet provides the cheapest and most extensive access to information on Indonesia. The addresses listed below are just starting places. Follow the links they provide, and you can go just about anywhere. Many Indonesia-related sites provide both Indonesian and English-language versions.

Internet Resources on Indonesia. http://www.auckland.ac.nz/asi/indo/links.html. Excellent starting point that includes recommended home pages, country information, universities in Indonesia, news, and more.

Indonesia: Environment and Development. hhttp://www.worldbank.org/html/ea3dr/exec.html. Provides information on Indonesia's forests, management of water resources, and the growing threat of urban and industrial pollution, and suggestions about what needs to be done.

Indonesian Homepage. http://indonesia.elga.net.id/. Includes basic country information, cultural pages, statistics, and more. Well-managed jumping-off point to many other sites.

Jendela Indonesia. http://www.lit.edu/(syafsya. Includes links to Indonesian newspapers and magazines (including English-language ones), Indonesian-English dictionary, and conversation, as well as travel information.

Windows to Indonesia and Asia Pacific Science and Technology. http://cc5.kuleuven.ac.be/ppi.leuven/indokul/asia/scietech.html. Links to research institutions, including the Indonesian Institute of Science (LIPI). Don't be misled by the name; important documentation can be reached via links at this site.

Videography

Prepared by David Pomery. All resources listed below are ¹/₂" VHS format unless otherwise noted.

Primary Resource

Indonesia: Rushing into Tomorrow

Sale:	$29.95	1997	28:30 min.
Rental:	$15.00		

Many North Americans have had little contact with Indonesia, but that is changing. Indonesia is making a giant leap from traditional culture to becoming part of the new international economy. With 200 million people—the world's fourth largest nation—in a country whose islands span a distance that equals that of New York to San Francisco, Indonesia is becoming a major player on the world stage. This video looks at some of the traditional sources of Indonesian culture to help us understand it better. It also considers some of the difficult problems the country faces, such as the status of East Timor. Although Indonesia is predominately Muslim, Christianity and other religions influence its culture and society. While Indonesia rushes toward industrialization, it still has many of the features of a traditional rural society, making a unique blend of old and new. Study guide included.

Available for sale only from
Friendship Press Distribution Office
P.O. Box 37844
Cincinnati, OH 45222-0844
(513) 948-8733

Available for rental only from
EcuFILM
810 Twelfth Avenue, South
Nashville, TN 37203
(800) 241-4091

Secondary Resources

Death of a Nation: The Timor Conspiracy

Sale:	$35.00	1994	76 min.

Controversy continues over Indonesia's role in East Timor. This powerful video (much of it filmed in secret) depicts people killed by the Indonesian military, a land dotted with graves, and the issues involved in the controversy, over the right of self-determination. The point is made that East Timor has little in common with Indonesia—it is predominantly Catholic and animistic, while Indonesia is predominantly Muslim. Produced by John Pilger.

> Available for <u>sale</u> <u>only</u> from
> East Timor Action Network
> P.O. Box 1182
> White Plains, NY 10602
> 914-428-7299
> FAX: 914-428-7383
> e-mail: cscheiner@igc.apc.org

NOTE: Above sale price is for <u>private use</u> only; for public performance rights the cost is $150

Learning from Borobudur

> Rental: $15.00   1989   35 min.

The Buddhist temple at Borobudur is 1,000 years old. This video allows the viewer to understand some of its secrets, as the camera follows the path of the pilgrims to the top of the structure and interprets the stories carved in stone. The video also helps us understand the process the pilgrims went through as they sought enlightenment. Many of the stories on Borobudur are still relevant and challenge present-day society. Study guide included.

> Available for <u>rental</u> <u>only</u> from
> EcuFILM [see above]

Love in Action

> Sale: $12.00   1989   15 min.

Produced by United Methodist Committee on Relief, this video looks at the plight of refugees in Indonesia, gives an overview of the demographics of the country, and visits local church projects to raise fish in Tulong and to build up a water supply. Locations: Java, Jakarta, southern Sumatra. Emphasis is on United Methodist projects, but on the whole this is an instructional overview that celebrates a quality of life.

> Available for <u>sale</u> <u>only</u> from
> EcuFILM [see above]

Silk and Steel

> Sale: $350
> Rental: $75   1997   56 min.

Women have begun to play key roles in reshaping the traditionally male-dominated culture of Indonesia, especially in relation to the economic boom and conflicting claims over human rights. Narrated by Indonesian television producer Sumita Tobing, this documentary looks at Sumita and her team making a program about the women who influence Indonesia. The program shows their obstacles and victories, enabling us to reflect "from the inside" on their successful combination of "silk and steel." Portraits include Denada, a rap star at sixteen who is also a devout Muslim, and Nursyahbani Katjasungkana, a lawyer who has been successful in prosecuting the first case of sexual harassment in the workplace.

> Available from
> Filmakers Library
> 124 E. 40th Street
> New York, NY 10016
> 212-808-4980
> FAX: 212-808-4983
> e-mail: info@filmakers.com